The Two Hundredth
Anniversary of
George Washington's
Inauguration

200 *G. Washington*

April 30, 1989

This book was published with the assistance of the New York State Commission on the Bicentennial of the United States Constitution and generous contributions by Mr. & Mrs. Milton Petrie and Mr. & Mrs. Zachary Fisher

FINAL REPORT OF THE NEW YO

Where the Experiment Began: New York City and the Two Hundredth Anniversary of George Washington's Inauguration

COMMISSION ON THE BICENTENNIAL OF THE CONSTITUTION

BY Richard B. Bernstein, HISTORIAN TO THE COMMISSION
WITH CONTRIBUTIONS BY MICHAEL T. FIUR, PETER NISSEN AND SHERI HORN
FOREWORD BY Joseph H. Flom, Esq., CHAIRMAN,
INTRODUCTION BY Peter S. Kohlmann, EXECUTIVE DIRECTOR,
AND Richard B. Bernstein
EDITED BY PETER S. KOHLMANN   DESIGNED BY JOAN STOLIAR

Dedication

Two members of the New York City Commission on the Bicentennial of the Constitution died before the commemoration of 1989. U.S. District Judge Edward Weinfeld (1901-1988) was probably the most distinguished trial judge in the history of the federal court system. His decades of active service on the federal bench were in the highest traditions of the American legal and constitutional system. Professor Richard B. Morris (1904-1989), Gouverneur Morris Professor Emeritus of History at Columbia University, was for more than sixty years one of the most prolific, wide-ranging, and eminent scholars in American history. An inspiring teacher who wrote and edited dozens of major works, Professor Morris also was one of the foremost contributors to the commemoration of the Bicentennial of the Constitution. Both Professor Morris and Judge Weinfeld were valued and esteemed members of the New York City Commission on the Bicentennial.
We dedicate this book to their memory.

Copyright © 1989 New York City Commission on the
Bicentennial of the Constitution.
All rights reserved. No part of this book may be reproduced in any form or
by any means without prior written permission of the New York City
Commission on the Bicentennial of the Constitution, 51 Chambers Street,
Rm. 525, New York, N.Y. 10077.

Library of Congress Cataloging-in-Publication Data available: LC card number 89-13817
ISBN 0-9625400-0-5

Designed & Produced by Joan Stoliar

Logo design by Ivan Chermayeff

Printed in the United States of America

The New York City Commission on the Bicentennial of the Constitution is deeply grateful to the following individuals and corporations who have made possible its programs and the creation of The Museum of American Constitutional Government at Federal Hall.

PRESIDENTIAL SPONSORS
Anheuser-Busch Companies, Inc.
Skadden, Arps, Slate, Meagher & Flom

INAUGURAL BENEFACTORS
The Carter Organization, Inc.
Drexel Burnham Lambert, Inc.
Kohlberg, Kravis, Roberts & Co.
May Department Stores Company
Morgan Stanley & Co., Incorporated
New York Stock Exchange, Inc.
Mr. and Mrs. Milton Petrie
Revlon Group Incorporated
Warner Communications Inc.

COMMEMORATIVE PATRONS
American Express Company
Capital Cities/ABC, Inc.
G O S L Acquisition Corp.
Gulf + Western Inc.

The Henley Group, Inc./
   Wheelabrator Technologies Inc.
Mead Data Central
E. John Rosenwald, Jr.

BICENTENNIAL PATRONS
Forbes Magazine
Mr. and Mrs. Rupert Murdoch
The Seamen's Bank for Savings
The Sharp Foundation
The Waldorf-Astoria
World Yacht Cruises

CONTRIBUTORS
Allen & Company Incorporated
Allied Signal Corporation
Amerada Hess Corp.
American Brands, Inc.
ASARCO Incorporated
CBS, Inc.
Caswell-Massey
The Chase Manhattan Bank, N.A.
Chemical Bank

Chermayeff & Geismar Associates
Colgate-Palmolive Company
Debevoise & Plimpton
Donald Drapkin
Ehrenkranz, Ehrenkranz & Schultz
Milton Glaser Associates
Jerome L. Greene Foundation
International Paper Co.
Estee Lauder Inc.
R.H. Macy & Co., Inc.
Manufacturers Hanover Corp.
Merrill Lynch
Metromedia Company
J.P. Morgan & Co. Incorporated
New York Community Trust
Paul, Weiss, Rifkind, Wharton
   & Garrison
Prudential-Bache Securities Inc.
Tiffany & Co.
Wasserstein, Perella & Co., Inc.
F.W. Woolworth Co.
Mr. and Mrs. William Wrigley

The President's Ball

GOLDEN CIRCLE BENEFACTORS
Bear, Stearns & Co. Inc.
Mme. Amalia de Fortabat
The Equitable Financial Companies
The First Boston Corporation
Zachary Fisher
Furman, Selz, Mager, Dietz & Birney
Kekst & Company, Inc.
Lazard Freres & Co.
Mr. and Mrs. Milton Petrie
Mac Schwebel
Reliance Group Holdings, Inc.
Revlon Group Incorporated
Skadden, Arps, Slate, Meagher & Flom/
   Mr. and Mrs. Joseph H. Flom
Wachtell, Lipton, Rosen & Katz
Warner Communications Inc.

SILVER PATRONS
C W Group and Friends
D.F. King & Co., Inc.
Dyson-Kissner-Moran Corporation
David Judelson
Loews Foundation
Manufacturers Hanover Corp.
Multinational Trading Company
Mr. and Mrs. Rupert Murdoch
Neuberger & Berman
Occidental Petroleum Corporation
Mr. and Mrs. Augustus K. Oliver
Mr. and Mrs. Laurance S. Rockefeller
Stephen C. Swid/SBK Entertainment
   World Inc.
Texaco Inc.
Donald J. Trump
Weil, Gotshal & Manges
Westvaco Corporation
Charles P. Young Company

SPONSORS
Mrs. Vincent Astor
Athlone Industries, Inc.
American International Group
Bauman Family Foundation
Donald Engel
General Host Corporation
Grey Advertising
The Interpublic Group of Companies, Inc.
ITT Corporation
Merrill Lynch Capital Markets
Neil F. Phillips
Potamkin Cadillac

Foreword

We New Yorkers are proud of our city and its rich history. New York's role as the nation's capital from 1784 through 1790 made the City the focal point for some of the most important stages in the creation of the United States Constitution, the government it authorized, and the Bill of Rights.

New Yorkers such as Alexander Hamilton and John Jay helped lead their fellow citizens, in the city and in the nation, in an unprecedented process of inventing a free government for a free people. As the New York City Commission on the Bicentennial reminded us during the bicentennial celebrations of 1987-89, the Constitution may have been written in Philadelphia, but New York was where the experiment began.

The commemoration of New York City's role in the making of the Constitution is a long and proud tradition in our city. Every fifty years, Presidents and former Presidents, dignitaries from nations around the world, and citizens from all walks of life help New Yorkers celebrate the anniversary of George Washington's inauguration as the first President. The 1989 celebration was a worthy milestone in that tradition.

Just as important, the bicentennial of 1987-89 gave us the opportunity to learn about the origins of our government and our most cherished liberties, and to learn the true meaning of our constitutional legacy. During that time, the City Commission on the Bicentennial sought not only to commemorate the history of the 1780s, but to remind us all that we have a *living* Constitution. The making of the Constitution is a political and legal process which continues to this day—a process in which all of us, not just lawyers and judges and scholars, play a vital part.

Two hundred years ago, Alexander Hamilton showed a foreign visitor into the gallery of the House of Representatives with the remark, "Here, sir, the people govern." The people still govern in 1989; the United States Constitution is the oldest written constitution still in effect anywhere in the world. But the American experiment which began here in the spring of 1789 can work only if we take seriously our rights and responsibilities as citizens. That was the central meaning of the 1989 commemoration of Washington's inauguration.

I hope that this handsome book chronicling the history of the 1780s and New York City's tradition of commemorating that history conveys that message, and that it will give its readers a renewed appreciation not only of the celebrations of 1989, but of why the events of 1789 deserve to be remembered.

Although the Acknowledgments section lists many of the men and women whose contributions to this commemorative project made it a great success, I think it appropriate to give special recognition here to Mayor Edward I. Koch. Mayor Koch recognized before anyone else the importance to this city of the bicentennial of the Constitution and of George Washington's inauguration. In 1986, Mayor Koch created the City Commission on the Bicentennial and defined its mandate. I was honored to accept the Mayor's invitation to chair the City Commission; as we close our business with the submission of this Report, I want to express my gratitude for his leadership and his support.

JOSEPH H. FLOM
Chairman
New York City Commission
on the Bicentennial of the Constitution

Washington's Triumphal Entry, 1783. Broadway, north from Fulton Street. Courtesy, Museum of the City of New York.

MESSAGE FROM

Sir Crispin Tickell GCMG KCVO

1789 was one of those years in which human history suddenly moved in new directions. The inauguration of George Washington as the first President of the United States was an event which marked such a departure. In one sense it grew out of the past and the heritage which Britain and the United States so conspicuously share; but in another it looked forward to 200 years of continuous, open, free and democratic government in the United States.

It was happy and right that my country should have been represented at the inauguration in 1789. In this fashion our two countries showed that they could put behind them their differences at the time, and distinguish what was important in the longer perspective. As British Permanent Representative to the United Nations, I felt honoured not only to participate personally but also to represent my country at this birthday in your national life. The values which the British and Americans share are well represented in the United Nations which our two countries helped to found almost 45 years ago. The United Nations, like the United States, is another experiment in the thinking and practice of policies we pursue in common. Let us hope that long before another 200 years have gone by, the ideals of the Charter, like the ideals in your own Constitution, will flourish and influence the international family of which we are a part.

PHOTOS: EDWARD REED

Introduction

On April 29-30, 1989, New Yorkers led the nation in marking the two hundredth anniversary of the inauguration of George Washington as the first President of the United States. This commemoration was the culmination of the work of the New York City Commission on the Bicentennial of the Constitution, created by Mayor Edward I. Koch in the fall of 1986 and chaired by Joseph H. Flom, Esq. This book recounts the history of the City Commission and its efforts to commemorate the bicentennials of the drafting and adoption of the Constitution and of the launching of the American experiment in constitutional government, focusing on New York's role in these major historical events. As both Mayor Koch and Chairman Flom reminded their fellow citizens, New York is where the experiment began.

★ ★ ★

Since 1976, New York City has played a major role in several national and local anniversaries, including the bicentennial of the declaration of American independence in 1976, the centennial of the Brooklyn Bridge in 1983, the centennial of the Statue of Liberty in 1986, and the bicentennials of the making of the Constitution in 1987-1989.

By contrast with these other anniversaries, those of the Constitution were not clearly focused in the public's attention. The reason is inherent in the origins of the Constitution. That document was the product of a political process spanning nearly twenty years. Unlike the dedication of a statue or a bridge, there was no one well-defined historical event on which the public imagination could focus. Unlike the beginning of the war for independence, the drafting, adoption, and implementation of a new form of government lacked a dramatic, symbolic act that could be the centerpiece of a public celebration.

The academic community had recognized this difficulty as early as 1976, when the American Political Science Association and the American Historical Association created Project '87. Chaired by Professors James MacGregor Burns of Williams College and Richard B. Morris of Columbia University, Project '87 sought not only to foster new scholarship on the history and principles of American constitutional government, but to encourage scholars to reach out to a wider audience.

The success of Project '87 set a model for other bicentennial programs, including that of the New York City Commission on the Bicentennial of the Constitution. As announced at its first formal press conference at Federal Hall National Memorial on April 30, 1987, the Commission's main purpose was to encourage awareness of and interest in the history and principles of the Constitution among the general public and, in particular, the schoolchildren of New York City.

The Commission sought to emphasize two principal themes:

★ First, New York City was where the experiment in constitutional government began. Although the Constitution was written in Philadelphia at the Federal Convention of 1787, and although it was ratified by the people of the United States in 1787 and 1788, it was not a self-executing charter of government. Those who wrote and supported it had to make it work, and that vital national effort took place in New York City, the first capital of the United States under the Constitution. New York City is where the first Congress under the Constitution convened; where that body declared George Washington elected as the first President of the United States; where the first President was inaugurated, and where the executive departments of government and the federal judiciary were created; and where the first constitutional amendments, the Bill of Rights, were drafted and proposed to the states.

★ Second, the Constitution is a *living* document. Its making did not end with its framing in Philadelphia in 1787, nor with its adoption in 1788, nor with the adoption of the Bill of Rights in 1791. It

continues to this day. This effort of what Benjamin Franklin called
"constitutional building" is not the sole province of lawyers and
judges, of legislators and politicians. It is in the hands of the
American people, encompassing those from all walks of life, of all
races, colors, and creeds, of both sexes and all religions.

This book describes the work of the City Commission on the Bicentennial and the various other activities and programs marking the Bicentennial in New York City. As with so many other aspects of the Commission's work, the need to prepare this history was suggested by the precedent set by the Committee of Citizens who organized the 1889 Centennial celebration and who sponsored the publication of Clarence Bowen's 1892 *History of the Centennial of the Inauguration of George Washington as First President of the United States*.

We hope that this book will be of use in the planning of future commemorations of the inauguration of George Washington, as the Bowen *Centennial History* was for us. We also offer this book as a contribution to the literature produced by specialists in American studies such as the late John William Ward, Merrill D. Peterson, Michael G. Kammen, Garry Wills, Barry Schwartz, Karal Ann Marling, and Paul K. Longmore. Their analyses of the changing reputations of historical figures and the ways in which the American people have commemorated significant national anniversaries have provided us with new ways to interpret American history, culture, and government. We hope that this book will add something of value to this continuing interpretative enterprise.

PETER S. KOHLMANN
Executive Director
New York City Commission
on the Bicentennial of the Constitution

RICHARD B. BERNSTEIN
Historian
New York City Commission
on the Bicentennial of the Constitution

Contents

SPONSORS   7

FOREWORD BY *Joseph H. Flom, Esq.*   8

MESSAGE FROM *Sir Crispin Tickell*   11

INTRODUCTION BY *Peter S. Kohlmann*
AND *Richard B. Bernstein*   12

Part One

1

Launching the Ship of State:
The Events of 1789

PAGE 20

2

Previous Commemorations in New York City
1839: Defending the Constitution and the Union
1889: The Constitution and the Union Triumphant
1939: The Forgotten Guest at the Sesquicentennial

PAGE 32

3

Organization and Preliminary Activities: 1987-1988

PAGE 44

Part Two

4
Preparing for the Bicentennial
Planning and Co-ordination
Promoting and funding the
Bicentennial *by Michael T. Fiur*

PAGE 52

5
Recreating Washington's Journey and
Arrival in New York City

PAGE 60

6
"The Presidency in the 90's"—The Fordham Symposium

PAGE 66

7
Saturday, April 29, 1989
Presidential Flotilla
Fireworks Spectacular

PAGE 76

8
Sunday, April 30, 1989
Commemorative Service at St. Paul's Chapel
Commemorative Inaugural Ceremony at Federal Hall
Bicentennial Procession
Presidential Descendants *by Peter Nissen*
The President's Ball at the Waldorf-Astoria

PAGE 86

9
The Legacy of the Bicentennial:
The Museum of American Constitutional Government

PAGE 118

10
The Bicentennial in Perspective

PAGE 123

APPENDIX A: MEMBERS AND STAFF OF THE COMMISSION 128
APPENDIX B: EXHIBITIONS AND SPECIAL PROGRAMS 130
APPENDIX C: DAIS GUESTS 132
ACKNOWLEDGEMENTS 133

Part One

"Poughkeepsie, N.Y.," pen and ink on paper by Alexander Robertson, 1796. New York's convention began meeting in Poughkeepsie on June 17, 1788. Although the Constitution's opponents outnumbered its supporters, 46 to 19, the delegates voted to ratify the Constitution on July 26, by a vote of 30 to 27. Courtesy, New York Historical Society.

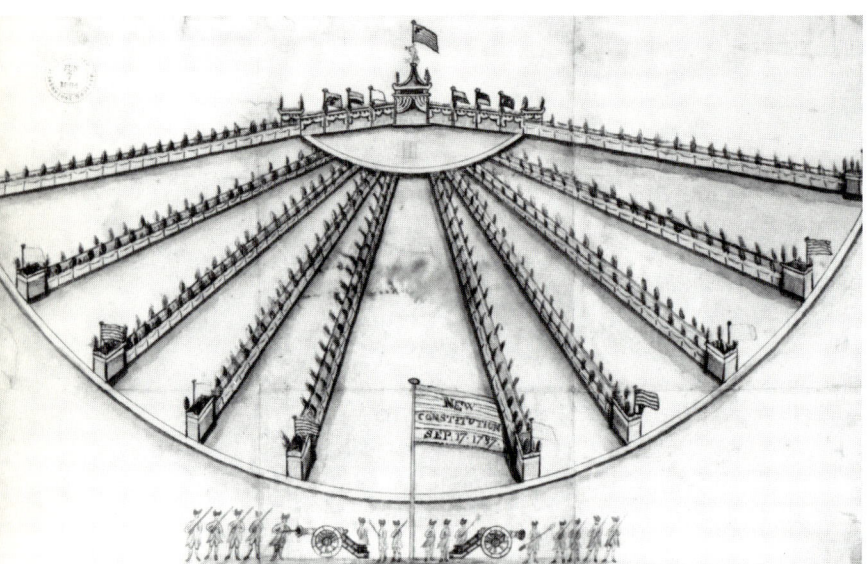

"Banquet Pavilion," watercolor by David Grim, undated. On July 23, 1788, more than five thousand people marched in a "Grand Federal Procession" to celebrate the news that ten states had ratified the proposed constituion, and also to put pressure on the Poughkeepsie convention. They then sat down to an enormous banquet under a pavilion. Major Pierre L'Enfant's design shows ten large tables, each representing one of the ratifying states, arranged in a rising sun pattern. Courtesy, New York Historical Society.

"The Eleventh Pillar," Massachusetts Centinel, August 2, 1788. A popular campaign device with the Constitution's supporters was the publication of newspaper cartoons depicting each ratification as the raising of another pillar in the "grand federal edifice." This cartoon shows New York's ratification, the last before the new government went into operation. Courtesy, New York Historical Society.

1

Launching the Ship of State: The Events of 1789

Federal Hall, The Seat of Congress. Line engraving by Amos Doolittle after Peter LaCour, 1790. Courtesy Stokes Collection, New York Public Library.

In 1789, two momentous events in the history of government took place: the launching of American constitutional government and the beginning of the French Revolution. The latter was more spectacular and dramatic, but the former's effects were just as significant. For the first time in world history, a people had chosen their own form of government and set out to make it work, defying the conventional wisdom that declared that human beings could not govern themselves.

★ ★ ★

The Constitution is not a self executing document. The Federal Convention of 1787, the body that wrote the Constitution, had no power to impose its work on the American people; instead, the proposed Constitution was submitted first to the Confederation Congress, and then to popularly elected ratifying conventions in each state. The people of the United States, represented in these conventions, thus were the first people in human history to choose how they were to govern themselves. After the adoption of the Constitution, the new charter of government had to be put into effect. This process took place in New York City, which had been the capital of the United States since 1785 and thus was the first capital of the new republic under the Constitution. (The selection of New York City occurred by default; the members of the Confederation Congress, unable to agree where the new capital should be, decided to leave it in New York City for the time being, leaving the final choice to the first Congress elected under the Constitution.)

The new home for the new government was a building at the corner of Wall, Broad, and Nassau Streets. Originally built in 1699-1701 as New York's City Hall, the structure had since 1785 hosted the Confederation Congress, and in turn had acquired the new name of Congress Hall. In 1788-89, leading private citizens such as John Jay and Alexander Hamilton raised funds to renovate and refurbish the building, which they then presented to the United States as Federal Hall. A Frenchman, Major Pierre Charles L'Enfant, supervised the renovation of Federal Hall. The city government meanwhile moved its operations to the old merchant's exchange, which stood in the middle of Broad Street, south of Fraunces Tavern.

Elections for the First Federal Congress took place through the winter of 1788-89 and the spring of 1789, as there was no uniform national election day. There were no political parties in the sense that we would recognize today; loosely-organized coalitions based on personal and local loyalties dominated the politics of each state, and national political issues strove with local concerns for dominance. The rivalries and hostilities from the controversy over ratification of the Constitution had not abated. For example, North Carolina and Rhode Island had not yet adopted the Constitution. And, because of bitter divisions in the New York legislature between supporters (Federalists) and diehard opponents (Anti-Federalists) of the Constitution, the state was not represented in the Senate until the summer of 1789.

At the same time, the states chose presidential electors who would have the responsibility for electing the first President and Vice President of the United States—though again New York did not choose electors, due to the state's continuing internal political strife. Under the original Electoral College (defined in Article II, Section 1 of the Constitution), the electors were to vote for two men, at least one of whom should not be from their own state. The candidate receiving the highest number of votes would become President; the runner-up would become Vice President. In 1789, it was clear to every informed political observer that George Washington was the clear favorite to become the first President of the United States.

The First Federal Congress, which had the task under the Constitution of counting the electoral votes and announcing the winners, was scheduled to convene in New York City on March 4, 1789. The day was greeted with the firing of cannon and the ringing of church bells, but, to the consternation of supporters of the Constitution, neither the House nor the Senate could muster a quorum. As days passed and Representatives and Senators straggled into New York City, observers worried whether the new Constitution would turn out to be no better than the discarded Articles of Confederation, whose Confederation Congress often could not muster a quorum to do business. On April 1, the House finally had a quorum; five days later, the Senate also mustered a quorum. On April 6, Congress met for its first joint session, and declared George Washington and John Adams elected as the first President and Vice President of the United States. They then named Charles Thomson, the Secretary of the old Confederation Congress, to carry the news to Washington; Benjamin Bourne (a pro-Constitution Rhode Islander who eventually represented his state in the House in the First Congress) was selected to inform John Adams of his election. Thomson left for Mount Vernon, and Bourne headed to Braintree, Massachusetts. Congress then returned to work—the House turning to the task of framing the first customs and tariff legislation, and the Senate to questions of ceremony and protocol.

As he waited for news of his election, Washington was not sure that he could handle the job—and he was virtually certain that he did not want it. He confided to his friend (and future Secretary of War) Henry Knox that his feelings on going to assume the Presidency were "not unlike those of a culprit going to the place of his execution." In fact, even after his election was all but certain, Alexander Hamilton and James Madison had to talk him out of a last-minute attack of cold feet. Washington's reluctance grew out of his genuine hope for a peaceful retirement, and his desire to disclaim ambitions unbecoming a gentleman assuming public trusts and responsibilities.

Washington received the news of his election when Thomson arrived at Mount Vernon on April 14. Two days later, he left his plantation, accompanied by Thomson and by Major David Humphreys, his longtime aide, for the journey through Virginia, Maryland, Delaware, Pennsylvania, and New Jersey to New York City. Although he was one of the wealthiest men in the United States, Washington was cash-poor, and had to borrow six hundred pounds from a neighbor to finance his journey and settle his debts. Martha Washington stayed behind, waiting for word from her husband as to when it would be best for her to join him. Thus, she missed the inauguration on April 30, not arriving in New York City until the end of May.

Washington chose to travel overland to observe the American people, and to gauge their opinion of the new Constitution and his election as President. The trip was an unbroken bout of patriotic celebration and of adulation for the fifty-seven-year-old Virginian. Town after town honored the "greatest man in the world" with fetes and ceremonies. Washington was relieved that the bitterness of the ratification controversy of 1787-1788 had passed, but he was alarmed at the extent of the people's faith in him—a faith that he did not share.

On April 23, 1789, the President-elect crossed New York Harbor in an elaborate barge, rowed by thirteen pilots from the New York Maritime Society. Dignitaries from Congress, the executive departments of the old Confederation, and the governments of New York State and New York City filled six other barges following Washington. The trip across the harbor must have given Washington an uneasy sense of the daunting tasks facing the new government. New Yorkers turned out in small sailing boats and along the shore to welcome him, but there were no American naval vessels; only a Spanish frigate, the *Galveston,* was on hand to fire a formal salute. Meanwhile, on April 21, John Adams had arrived from Braintree, uncertain as to what his job as Vice President was to be and still angry that he had been elected with one vote less than a majority of the votes cast by the first Electoral College.

For a week, as Washington waited and conferred with members of the House and the Senate, the plans for the inauguration took shape. The chief stumbling block was the ongoing quarrel between the House and the Senate over questions of protocol. The Senators, under the leadership of Vice President Adams, had conceived a passion for titles of office and a formal ceremony—a taste not shared by the House. The question of titles persisted for weeks after the inauguration. When the Senate proposed such titles for Washington as "His Elective Highness" or "His High Mightiness the President of the United States of America and Protector of their Liberties," the House

First in Peace, engraving by John C. McRae, 1857. Washington arrived at the Battery in New York City on April 23, 1789 in a lavishly decorated barge. Photograph courtesy of the Mount Vernon Ladies' Association.

Chancellor Robert R. Livingston, oil on canvas by Ezra Ames, 1814. Because there were as yet no federal judges, Livingston, chief judge of New York's equity courts and the state's highest ranking judge, administered the oath of office.

freezingly pointed out that the Constitution forbade titles of nobility and specified that the chief executive was to be called "the President of the United States." Vice President Adams lamented that there were presidents of fire companies and cricket clubs and predicted that sailors from foreign nations would show no respect for a mere President of the United States and would "despise him to all eternity."

As the Senate took the lead in planning the inaugural ceremonies, dazzled by the prospect of creating the republican equivalent of a coronation, Senator William Maclay of Pennsylvania watched sourly. Maclay, a plainspoken farmer and lawyer, revered Washington; he had protested indignantly against the Senate's taste for titles and ceremony, declaring that Washington needed no titles to be ranked as the first man in the world. Disgusted by his colleagues' obsession with ceremony, Maclay began to keep a diary as a record of what he saw and heard and a safe place to confide his acerbic commentary. Newly published in an accurate scholarly edition, the Maclay Diary is our principal firsthand account of the inauguration.

On April 30, the great day itself, the Senate still had not established the final shape of the ceremonies—or so Vice President Adams maintained. How, he asked, should the Senate receive the House of Representatives and the new President—standing or sitting? As the Senators wasted time and energy batting the question back and forth, the delegation of Senators who were to escort Washington to his inauguration forgot to leave, delaying the entire ceremony for more than an hour. Finally, the House, led by Speaker Frederick A. Muhlenberg of Pennsylvania, marched into the chamber. They were soon joined by the major participants, George Washington and Chancellor Robert R. Livingston, who had been escorted to Federal Hall by a dignified military procession.

Washington was dressed in a suit of brown American-made broadcloth, to indicate his support for American industries and his belief that he was taking office as a civilian rather than as the former commander-in-chief of the Continental Army. Because there were as yet no federal judges, Chancellor Livingston, the chief judge of the state's equity courts and New York's highest-ranking judge, was to administer the oath of office. These men, accompanied by Vice President Adams, Governor George Clinton of New York, and members of the House and Senate, stepped out onto the second-floor balcony of Federal Hall.

Crowds of New Yorkers filled the streets surrounding the building. They cheered loudly at their first sight of Washington, and the dignitaries waited for the celebrations to subside. Then Washington and Livingston stepped forward, only to discover that nobody had thought to bring a Bible to the ceremony. A messenger was hastily sent to a nearby Masonic lodge to borrow their Bible (Washington and most of the other participants in the ceremony were members of this fraternal order).

Washington repeated the constitutional oath of office after Livingston in a loud, firm voice: "I do solemnly swear that I will faithfully execute the Office of President of the United States, and will to the best of my Ability, preserve, protect and defend the Constitution of the United States." He then added, "So help me God," and bent forward to kiss the Bible. Livingston then shouted to the crowd, "Long live George Washington, President of the United States!" In so doing, Livingston echoed the traditional cry of welcome for a newly crowned British monarch. The people did not notice this "trapping of monarchy." They gave three cheers, which mingled with the ringing of church bells and the roar of cannon fired to mark the occasion.

Washington and the other dignitaries then returned to the Senate chamber, where the new President read the first inaugural address in American history. Washington had scrapped his seventy-five-page draft and instead delivered a short address of about twenty minutes. Some controversy exists about the authorship of Washington's speech; Irving Brant, James Madison's leading biographer, maintained that Madison had drafted the speech at his friend's request, but his claim has been challenged in recent years.

The substance of the President's speech was clear and simple: Washington lamented his lack of qualifications, acknowledged and invoked the blessings of Providence, endorsed the new Constitution, and disclaimed any purpose to direct Congress in its legislative responsibilities. In all this, the President was careful to adhere to the prevailing conception of the Presidency as a nonpartisan executive office; the President would be the republican equivalent of the king of Great Britain, representing the interests of the whole people of the United States and seeking to advance and promote the general good. Moreover, Washington shared the general belief in this period that Congress was the center of gravity of the constitutional system, and that Congress therefore had the principal responsibility for formulating public policy.

Nonetheless, Washington did choose to comment on one major issue facing the new government—that of proposed amendments to the Constitution. He knew that the Anti-Federalists

Inauguration of Washington, engraving after Chappel, 1859. Washington was inaugurated as first President on April 30, 1789 on the balcony of Federal Hall in New York City. Photography courtesy of the Mount Vernon Ladies' Association.

This Masonic Bible was the one on which Washington was sworn in as the first President. Both Washington and Livingston, as well as other members of the new government, were members of this civic and fraternal order.

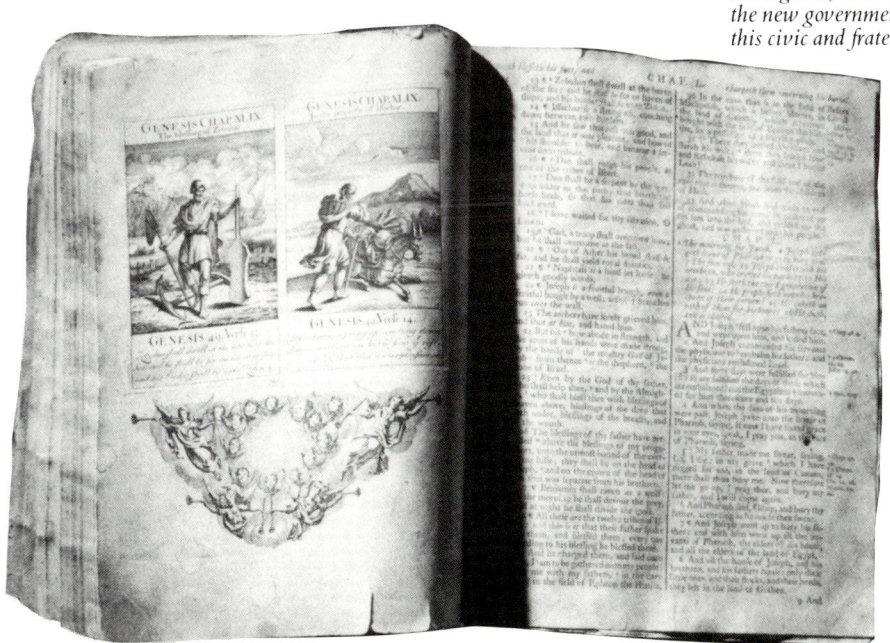

had not given up their opposition to the form of government created by the Constitution; rather, they had shifted their ground, seeking by amendment to sap the powers of the new government to regulate commerce and to enact taxes and customs regulations. Moreover, many Anti-Federalists and indeed many Federalists had demanded that the Constitution be amended to include a declaration of rights to limit the powers of the government of the United States. The lack of a bill of rights had been the single most powerful argument against the Constitution in the ratification controversy of 1787-1788, and the President was determined, along with Madison and other moderate Federalists, to defuse this objection. Washington thus endorsed the call for amendments, but carefully defined the kinds of amendments that he believed desirable:

> *Instead of undertaking particular recommendations on this subject, in which I could be guided by no lights derived from official opportunities, I shall again give way to my entire confidence in your discernment and pursuit of the public good. For I assure myself that whilst you carefully avoid every alteration which might endanger the benefits of an United and effective Government, or which ought to await the future lessons of experience, a reverence for the characteristic rights of freemen, and a regard for the public harmony, will sufficiently influence your deliberations on the question how far the former can be more impregnably fortified or the latter be safely and advantageously promoted.*

Washington then refused any salary, expressing the hope that Congress simply would consent to pay his expenses, as the Continental Congress had done when he became commander-in-chief of the Continental Army in 1775. Perhaps remembering the staggering total at the end of Washington's detailed 1775-1783 expense account, Congress persisted in adopting a presidential salary instead of agreeing to pay his expenses.

The content of Washington's speech was guaranteed to win the approval of Congress, but his manner surprised and pained his audience. Senator Maclay has left us the best eyewitness account:

> *[T]his great Man was agitated and embarrassed more than ever he was by the levelled Cannon or pointed Musket. He trembled, and several times could scarce make out to read, though it must be supposed he had often read it before. He put part of the fingers of his left hand, into the side, of what I think the Taylors call the fall, of his Breeches. Changing the paper into his left hand, after some time, he then did the same with some of the fingers of his right hand. When he came to the Words all the World, he made a flourish with his right hand, which left rather an ungainly impression. I sincerely, for my part, wished all set ceremony in the hands of the dancing Masters, and that this first of Men, and read off, his address, in the plainest Manner without ever taking his Eyes From the paper, for I felt hurt, that he was not first in everything.*

After the President finished his speech, he and the House and Senate adjourned to nearby St. Paul's Chapel for a religious service; Maclay had recorded his discontent at this proposal, blaming the "churchmen" (that is, Episcopalians) in the Senate. That evening, the finest display of fireworks and illuminations yet seen in the United States took place in New York City to celebrate the launching of the new government.

★ ★ ★

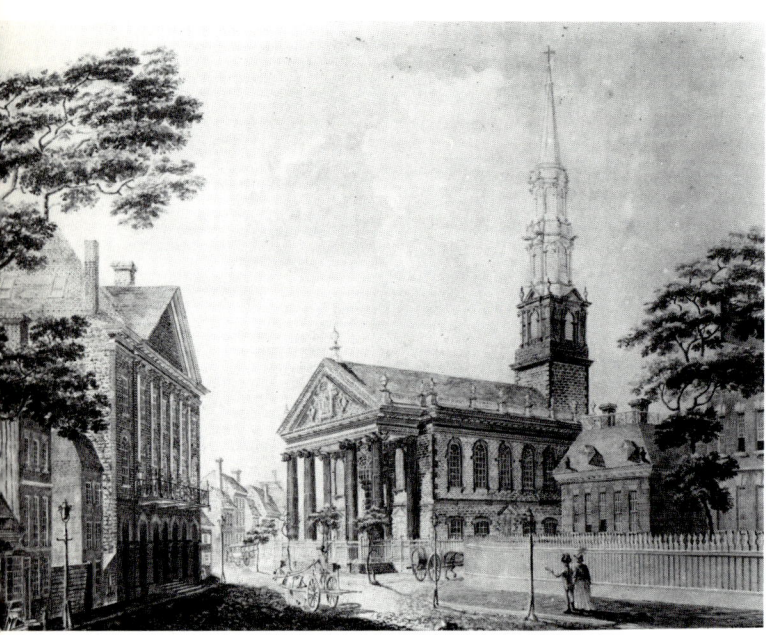

St. Paul's Chapel as depicted in a watercolor by C. Milbourne. The Chapel in the oldest public building and the only structure still standing from the days of the early national period.

During the rest of 1789, Congress played the principal role in the new national government. Under the leadership of Representative James Madison of Virginia, the House dominated the legislative work of Congress. The only major pieces of legislation originating in the Senate were the Judiciary and Process Acts of 1789, the statutes organizing the federal court system. The House originated all the other major statutes enacted by Congress—among them the laws establishing the first executive departments (State, Treasury, and War), the first tariff, customs, and appropriations measures. In addition, Madison carried out a promise that he had made in the heat of the controversy over the Constitution in 1787-1788: he spearheaded the campaign to propose constitutional amendments protecting individual rights. Despite opposition from some Federalists who thought them unnecessary, and others who charged that Madison was bidding for popularity, and Anti-Federalists who maintained that Madison's proposals did not go far enough, Congress ultimately proposed twelve constitutional amendments to the states in September of 1789. Ten of these were ratified by enough states to become part of the Constitution; we know these first ten amendments as the Bill of Rights. (The other two amendments—one setting up a complex and unworkable system of reapportioning the House of Representatives, the other forbidding pay increases for members of Congress until after a later election to Congress—were not ratified.)

President Washington's principal responsibilities were to review legislation proposed by Congress before signing it into law, to fill offices created by the statutes establishing the executive and judicial branches, and to serve as Head of State, or the ceremonial leader of the new nation. Both in that first year of office and throughout his two terms as the nation's first President, Washington had the tasks of making the Presidency work as an institution of government; of working with the other executive departments, with Congress, and with the federal courts to make the Constitution work as a charter of government; and of preserving the confidence of the American people in their experiment in government.

The first President was already sensitive to one of the most difficult tasks confronting any President: the ceremonial role of Head of State. Although he often found this symbolic role painful and embarrassing, Washington gamely bore the burden. In his conduct as President, he sought to maintain his personal dignity and reserve in the hope that it would come to be associated with the office he held, so that the personal respect he enjoyed would also attach itself to the Presidency. In particular, he followed the advice of his longtime adviser Alexander Hamilton, who maintained that pomp and ceremony were necessary to preserve the respect of the people for their chief executive. Other Americans, who feared that these "monarchical" trappings might dazzle the people into forgetting that they had once overthrown a monarch, criticized Washington for assuming kingly airs and for condoning the ornate ceremony of formal receptions, known as *levees*. Nonetheless, when the President journeyed throughout the northern states in October 1789, and on later tours of the middle and southern states, he was greeted with the same joy and celebrations that marked his April trip to New York City to become President. These outpourings of love and admiration reassured Washington about his conduct as President and about the Constitution's chances for success.

Washington found one of his other major responsibilities in 1789—to fill offices created by Congress—especially burdensome. As he explained to one friend:

That part of the President's duty which obliges him to nominate persons for office is the most delicate and in many instances will be, to me, the most unpleasing, for it may frequently happen that there will be several applicants for the same office, whose merits and pretensions are so nearly equal that it will almost require the aid of supernatural intuition to fix upon the right.

Washington governed his appointments policy by reference to three criteria. First, he sought the ablest men available. Second, he preferred to appoint those whom he knew to be warm friends of the Constitution and sincerely committed to its success. Third, aware of the touchy sensibilities of the several states and sections of the United States, he strove for geographic balance in his appointments to national office.

Washington devoted great care to selecting his principal advisers, the heads of the executive departments created by Congress. He regarded as a mandate of his office the part of Article II, Section 2 of the Constitution authorizing the President to require the written opinions of the heads of executive departments on major questions, and he convened them regularly to discuss pending issues. This practice gave rise to the first major extraconstitutional institution, the President's Cabinet (a term borrowed from British usage), then composed of the Secretaries of State, the Treasury, and War, and the Attorney General. The President also consulted Representative Madison (on whom he had come to rely during the framing and adoption of the Constitution) and Chief Justice John Jay.

Washington's habit of seeking advice from all available sources became a sore point with his critics, who charged that he was indecisive. A more accurate assessment came from his first Secretary of State, Thomas Jefferson, who declared long after Washington's death that the President's mind was "slow in operation, being little aided by invention or imagination, but sure in conclusion."

At one point in his first term, in pursuit of advice, Washington inadvertently set a major precedent in the area of separation of powers. He and Secretary of State Jefferson sought to submit a question of treaty interpretation to the Supreme Court, seeking what we would call an "advisory opinion." The justices of state supreme courts in Massachusetts and New Hampshire regularly gave—and continue to give—advisory opinions of this sort, but the U.S. Supreme Court was another matter. The Justices politely but firmly refused, declaring that their powers extended only to actual "cases or controversies," as required by Article III of the Constitution. (This did not prevent Chief Justice Jay from serving as a regular informal adviser to the President.)

Similarly, when Washington and Secretary of War Henry Knox came to the Senate in person to seek the advice and consent of the Senate to a proposed strategy for negotiating a treaty with Indian tribes, the Senators declined. Some were embarrassed and ill at ease; others believed that Washington had come to the Senate chamber to overawe the Senators into complying with his plans and wishes. An angered Washington muttered, "This defeats every purpose of my coming here!" and stalked from the chamber. The incident left no lingering hard feelings, but was the root of the understanding that negotiating a treaty falls within the province of the executive branch, with the Senate's role limited to ratifying or rejecting all or part of what the executive has been able to win through negotiation.

The President tended to defer to Congress in the shaping of federal policy, exercising his veto power only when he believed a proposed statute to be unconstitutional. As to economic issues, he permitted Treasury Secretary Hamilton great discretion, largely due to his confidence in Hamilton's knowledge and ability. On the other hand, he acted as his own Secretary of State and Secretary of War, believing that he had adequate experience and knowledge to assume those responsibilities. This tendency caused few problems for Secretary Knox, who resumed his familiar habit of executing Washington's instructions as he had done during the Revolution. However, Thomas Jefferson, one of the nation's most experienced diplomats, chafed at the degree to which, as Secretary of State, he was forced to follow the dictates of the President rather than have a free hand in shaping policy.

Few men could have managed to hold together a cabinet containing members as brilliant and antithetical as Hamilton and Jefferson. More than once, the President had to resort to cajolery and even to formal reprimands to control the antagonism that threatened to split his government. He tended to sympathize with Hamilton's points of view, for he shared with Hamilton firsthand knowledge of the weaknesses that had nearly destroyed the United States under the Articles of Confederation, as well as a pessimism about human nature lurking just underneath the calm face he showed to the world.

In addition, the President was alarmed by the rivalry and dissension between Hamilton and Jefferson because it hinted at an ominous development in the nation at large—the rebirth of party strife. Washington viewed the growing rupture between the Administration's supporters, or Federalists, and its opponents, or Republicans, as the first signs of factional conflict that might tear the republic to pieces. This had been the teaching of political philosophers and historians of republican government for thousands of years, and virtually every leading member of the Revolutionary generation shared these views. Despite their fears, however, the American political system adapted to the development of political parties, and the republic did not fall.

★ ★ ★

Although government under the Constitution began in New York City, within a year the new government left its birthplace. The decision to relocate the nation's temporary capital and the fight over where the permanent capital should be was the product of fierce political conflict and shrewd political deal-making.

During the summer of 1790, as controversy grew over Treasury Secretary Hamilton's fiscal proposals, another issue shared the center stage of American politics: the location of the permanent national capital. During the Revolution and the Confederation periods, the Continental and Confederation Congresses had had to move from city to city, sometimes on the run from British soldiers, sometimes because of squabbles between federal and local authorities. The framers of the Constitution agreed that it was vital for the new government to have a home under its

George Washington, oil on canvas by James Peale after Charles Willson Peale, ca. 1788. This portrait shows the first President as he looked on April 30, 1789, when he was inaugurated at Federal Hall in New York City. Photography courtesy of The New York Public Library, Astor, Lenox and Tilden Foundations.

The interior at Federal Hall (1789-1812), after drawing of the Senate Chamber by William Hindley, ca. 1930.

own control, but bypassed the interesting question of choosing the actual site. And, as we have seen, the Confederation Congress could not reach a decision either. Thus, the decision awaited the action of the First Congress, and in turn the issue became a central one in the politics of 1790.

Despite the hopes of New Yorkers, their city was destined to lose its status as the capital, for almost no one except New Yorkers wanted to keep the capital there. Senators and Representatives from southern states disliked New York, because it took so long to reach that city and because they felt that its atmosphere of commerce, trade, manufacturing, and speculating would prejudice the making of laws and policies against the needs of the southern agricultural states. New Englanders were willing to tolerate New York for the time being, but they joined with those from the middle states in preferring Philadelphia, the nation's largest and most modern city. Philadelphia had the advantage of a central location between North and South. Southerners disliked the strong antislavery views of many of the city's inhabitants, and regarded Philadelphia as only slightly less dominated by trade and commerce than New York.

It is still not clear how the decisions were made, or who the key participants were, but we do know that in June of 1790, a complex series of deals took place which historians have come to call the "Compromise of 1790." Under this compromise, it was agreed that Representatives and Senators from Virginia and other key states would abate their opposition to Hamilton's fiscal proposals; in return, it was agreed that Philadelphia would become the new temporary capital of the nation from 1790 to 1800, and that thereafter a permanent capital would be founded on the banks of the Potomac River between Virginia and Maryland.

★★★

By the late summer of 1790, when the federal government left New York for its new home in Philadelphia, the Revolutionary generation had succeeded in rechanneling American politics within the matrix of the Constitution. Moreover, the new machinery of government was steadily winning the acceptance and loyalty of the American people. New York City was the scene of several of the critical first steps in this process.

Although the city lost the prized status of national capital, it benefitted both from the government's short stay there and from the policies put into effect during 1789-1790. New York City was well on its way to becoming one of the wealthiest, liveliest, and most important urban centers of the United States. Its people's preoccupation with trade and commerce continued, augmenting the city's wealth, stimulating its growth and modernization.

The nation and the city grew side-by-side, and the events of 1789 were vital to both of them.

Sperm whale's tooth engraved with portrait of Washington. Inscribed "J. Hayden, N.Y./Feb. 1861." Long after his death, Washington was a powerful symbol for the American people. One foreign traveler commented in 1815: "Every American considers it his sacred duty to have a likeness of Washington in his home, just as we have the images of God's saints." Courtesy, the Museum of the City of New York.

Long Live The President: Recently unearthed at Clermont, Chancellor Livingston's estate in the Hudson River Valley, this rare button, made of gilt copper alloy, may have been worn by him at the 1789 inauguration.

JUBILEE OF THE CONSTITUTION.

A DISCOURSE.

When in the epic fable of the first of Roman Poets, the Goddess mother of Æneas delivers to him the celestial armour, with which he is to triumph over his enemy, and to lay the foundations of Imperial Rome, he is represented as gazing with intense but confused delight on the crested helm that vomits golden fires —

Portrait by Philip Haas, of former President John Quincy Adams. He was defeated for re-election by Andrew Jackson in 1828 but returned to public life in 1830, winning election to the U.S. House of Representatives from Massachusetts. He served there until his death. Adams spoke for two hours at the Cedar Street Baptist Church at the fiftieth anniversary of Washington's inauguration. Above is a reprint of the first passages of Adam's address. Courtesy, Library of Congress.

2

Previous Commemorations in New York City

COMMEMORATING the inauguration of George Washington and the launching of government under the Constitution has been a proud and venerable tradition in New York City. The jubilee (1839), centennial (1889), and sesquicentennial (1939) anniversaries of the events of 1789 were occasions for elaborate ceremonies expressing the values and preoccupations of their times.

1839: Defending the Constitution and the Union

The fiftieth anniversary of Washington's inauguration—"the jubilee of the Constitution"—occurred at a turning point of American political history. The last of the framers of the Constitution, James Madison of Virginia, had died three years before. Though his death in 1836 was not as spectacular in its impact on the popular imagination as the deaths of John Adams and Thomas Jefferson on July 4, 1826 (the fiftieth anniversary of the Declaration of Independence), Madison's passing was widely interpreted as marking the end of the "era of the Fathers." The founding generation of American politicians had departed, leaving their handiwork in the possession of a new generation whose members worried whether they could preserve the legacy entrusted to them.

Political events of the period only exacerbated their self-doubts. In 1832-1833, the legislature of South Carolina denounced a newly-enacted federal tariff as discriminating against the legitimate interests of the state. The South Carolina legislature asserted that the Constitution was an agreement, or compact, among the several states, and that the federal government was the creature of the state governments. Under the Constitution, advocates of the "state compact" theory maintained, a state legislature had the constitutional right and duty to declare a federal law unconstitutional and to void, or *nullify,* its operation within that state. The South Carolina legislature then nullified the 1828 "tariff of abominations," which levied import taxes on goods especially in demand within the state.

The nullification crisis pitted Senator (and former Vice President) John C. Calhoun of South Carolina, perhaps the ablest political thinker of the time and the principal theorist of nullification, against President Andrew Jackson of Tennessee, a firm believer in both state sovereignty and the sanctity of the Union. The nullification crisis, averted at the last moment by a compromise brokered by Senator Henry Clay of Kentucky, posed in starkest terms the controversy over the character of the Union; historians have agreed in terming it a prologue to the Civil War.

In consequence, the celebration of the fiftieth anniversary of Washington's inauguration became an occasion for New Yorkers to assert their commitment to a theory of the Constitution and its origins sharply distinct in character from Calhoun's "state compact" theory. The principal event was organized by the New York Historical Society, which itself had been formed in 1804 by staunch Federalists such as Gouverneur Morris (the draftsman of the Constitution, and the Society's first President) and Rufus King (a transplanted son of Massachusetts, and one of New York's first two Senators). As was the custom in the early nineteenth century, the principal feature of the commemoration was a long formal lecture—a "historical discourse."

The lecturer and guest of honor was himself a veteran defender of the Constitution and the Union: Representative John Quincy Adams of Massachusetts. Born in 1769, Adams was almost seventy years old, and midway through the last and greatest phase of his long political career. More than thirty years before, as a Senator from Massachusetts, he had defied his party and his state to support the policies of the Jefferson administration and to resist conservative Federalists' drift towards secession. As President from 1825 to 1829, Adams had unsuccessfully championed a vigorous national government and wide-ranging policies for national economic development. The first former President to resume an active political career after leaving office, Adams was embroiled in fierce controversies over slavery and the character of the Union. Adams welcomed the chance to restate his understanding of the origins of the Constitution and the Union, especially in honor of a President whom he revered as the greatest figure in American history. (Ironically, Adams's father, Washington's Vice President and successor as President, had a much lower and more sardonic estimation of George Washington.)

Adams spoke for two hours at the Cedar Street Baptist Church, his text embellished with classical references and quotations from Shakespeare and the Romantic poets. The story he told his enthralled audience was an uncompromisingly nationalist one: The People of the United States, acting as a unit, had made and adopted the Constitution; in the process, they had created a national government independent of and supreme over the state governments, one creating a permanent and glorious Union of the states. The emblem and incarnation of this national government and the Union was George Washington, the one American of his time immune to purely local loyalties. Washington's legacy to his countrymen and to posterity was an energetic, smoothly functioning national government, one standing for the twin principles of liberty and union. Adams concluded by exhorting his audience to preserve and extend this constitutional legacy, to resist the specter of disunion and defend the just powers of the national government. The toasts presented at the dinner that followed Adams's "discourse" restated and developed the orator's themes, implicitly refuting the constitutional "heresies" circulating south of the Mason-Dixon line.

In 1839, as the arguments of Calhoun and his allies clashed with those of John Quincy Adams at the "jubilee of the Constitution," acute observers might have concluded that, fifty years after the adoption of the Constitution, two starkly different constitutional traditions were developing, each with its own sectional base, each with its own cluster of heroes (in the South, Thomas Jefferson, John C. Calhoun; in the North, Alexander Hamilton, John Marshall, Henry Clay, Daniel Webster, and John Quincy Adams). And yet, despite—or, perhaps because of—their disagreements, both camps insisted on claiming Washington as one of their own. In the face of such profound controversy over such basic questions as the nature of the Union, the character of the Constitution, and the proper relationship between the state and federal governments, it was not surprising that some Americans began to despair of the survival of the Constitution and the Union.

1889: The Constitution and the Union Triumphant

The observance of the centennial on April 29 and 30 and May 1, 1889 was one of the greatest patriotic celebrations ever seen in the United States. Examining the Centennial of 1889 yields revealing insights into the nature of American society as the nation completed its first century of constitutional government.

The agenda of the 1889 centennial celebrations was crowded and potentially controversial, though the centennial planners were desperate to avoid controversy:

★ The first major national anniversary following the end of Reconstruction, the Centennial was an opportunity to dramatize the healing of sectional conflict that had given rise to the Civil War, and to celebrate the rise of the United States as a world-class industrial and military power. (The centennial of the signing of the Constitution in 1887 was ruined by localist squabbling among Philadelphia, New York, and Washington, D.C., all of which claimed the anniversary. President Grover Cleveland of New York was so indignant at the Philadelphia committee's local chauvinism that he put off to the last minute his agreement to participate in the celebrations in September 1887.)

★ The Centennial carried considerable political freight as well. President Benjamin Harrison, who had won election in 1888 with a majority of electoral votes even though his predecessor, Grover Cleveland, had outpolled him in the popular vote, seized on the centennial as an opportunity to bolster his legitimacy in the eyes of the American voters.

★ Finally, the centennial of Washington's inauguration was the occasion for a tug-of-war over patriotic symbolism pitting the wealthy against the poor and the descendants of colonial and Revolutionary families against recent immigrants.

★ ★ ★

On March 4, 1884, plans to observe the Centennial began with resolutions adopted by a formal meeting at The New York Historical Society; as in 1839, the Society took the initiative in targeting the anniversary as worthy of commemoration. Similar resolutions were adopted by the New York Society of the Sons of the Revolution in 1885 and the New York Chamber of Commerce in 1886.

The Committee of Citizens, which became the focus and organizer of Centennial planning, was itself organized at a meeting at the Fifth Avenue Hotel on November 10, 1887, presided over by the Mayor of New York City, Abram S. Hewitt. Mayor Hewitt appointed an executive committee of thirteen citizens, known as the Committee of Thirteen, which co-ordinated activities with the committees of The New York Historical Society, the Chamber of Commerce, and the Sons of the Revolution. On December 7, 1887, these groups merged into the Committee of Citizens, which then conducted its activities and prepared and carried out its plans as a unified body.

The Committee of Citizens (which sometimes termed itself the "General Committee") appointed eleven committees from its membership: Plan and Scope, States, General Government, Army (Military and Industrial Parade), Navy, Entertainment, Finance, Railroads and Transportation, Art, Exhibition, and Literary Exercises. (Art and Exhibition were later merged as one committee.) As noted in the official history of the Centennial observances, "So great was the pressure to join the General Committee, that the number was finally limited to two hundred."

The Finance Committee undertook to raise $175,000—$75,000 from New York City, $55,000 from New York State, and $45,000 from private fundraising. New York State appropriated a total of $200,000 to help defray the cost of the commemoration—$55,000 as requested by the Finance Committee, $125,000 for the National Guard, and $20,000 for the Grand Army of the Republic (the veterans of the U.S. Army in the Civil War.) To put these figures in modern terms, one 1889 dollar equals about $10-15 in 1989 purchasing power.

The Centennial celebrations focused on the three days of the weekend of the Centennial anniversary (April 29 through May 1, 1889). Two events sponsored by the Committee of Citizens served as a prelude and complement to its main program:

★ An exhibition of historical portraits and artifacts from the period 1776-1789 was organized in the spring of 1888 and was held for six weeks in the old Metropolitan Opera House, opening to the public on April 3, 1889.

★ A commemorative banquet sponsored by the Society of the Cincinnati was held at the Lawyers' Club in the old Equitable Building on the evening of April 27, 1889. One of the guests of honor was former President Rutherford B. Hayes of Ohio.

President Benjamin Harrison and Vice President Levi P. Morton (a native New Yorker) played leading roles in the events of the Centennial. Joining them and former Presidents Hayes and Cleveland were representatives of the U.S. Supreme Court (including the newly-appointed Chief Justice, Melville W. Fuller of Maine), delegations from the House of Representatives and the Senate, members of Harrison's Cabinet (representing the executive departments of the federal government), the diplomatic corps, and delegations from every state in the Union (including, in most cases, the states' governors).

The federal government's delegation, led by Harrison and Morton, made a ceremonial trip from Washington, D.C. to New York City. They had intended to follow exactly the route taken by George Washington in April 1789, but constraints of time forced them to abridge the schedule. They departed in a special train from Washington, D.C., on the evening of April 28, 1889, and arrived in Elizabeth, New Jersey, on the morning of April 29. This town was picked because George Washington had departed from Elizabethtown (as it was then named) for New York City a century before.

The first major event of the Centennial was the President's reprise that morning of Washington's trip across New York Harbor (on the morning of April 23, 1789). After a breakfast with Governor Robert S. Green of New Jersey, the Presidential party was conducted by military escort to Elizabethport. The U.S.S. *Despatch* picked up the Presidential party (a second steamer, the U.S.S. *Sirius,* took on others who could not be accommodated on the *Despatch*). A barge (replicating that which carried Washington across the harbor in 1789), crewed by shipmasters of the New York Marine Society, the same organization that had conducted Washington, met the *Despatch*. President Harrison and Vice President Morton transferred to the barge to be rowed across the harbor to the foot of Wall Street, landing at what was then Pier 16 (renumbered since then as the present-day Pier 11).

The harbor swarmed with ships and boats of every size and description. A grand Naval Parade divided into two sections—Naval and Merchant Marine—was the centerpiece of the morning. The Naval Parade included the cruisers U.S.S. *Chicago,* U.S.S. *Boston,* and U.S.S. *Yorktown,* and the steamers U.S.S. *Atlanta,* U.S.S. *Juniata,* and U.S.S. *Yantic,* followed by a procession of revenue cutters and yachts. The Merchant Marine section comprised about three hundred ships of all types (mostly river and harbor steamers), organized into 23 divisions of 13 ships each; these divisions were formed into three Grand Divisions, each commanded by a "Commodore." Great attention was paid to the arrangement of types of vessels, the "dressing" of all ships and boats, and the use of signals, whistles, and other formalities in both parts of the Naval Parade. As has become traditional in events in New York harbor, the steam tugs also saluted the President and Vice President as they were rowed across the harbor. They were received on Manhattan by the chairman of the Committee of Citizens, Hamilton Fish, and by Governor David B. Hill of New York and Mayor Hugh L. Grant of New York City. The official Centennial history commented:

> *Never before in the history of the United States had so many vessels been assembled at once in any of its ports to participate in any celebration. Steamers came from many places on the Hudson and Long Island Sound and on the Atlantic seaboard, laden with persons desirous of witnessing the naval review; but amid all the thousands on the waters of New York Bay during that fair day, not an accident occurred to mar the general joy. How different the sight from that of a century before, when President Washington came from Elizabethport in a barge through the Kill Van Kull. Then the United States had no navy, and the only naval salutes fired were from the Spanish corvette Galveston and a merchant-ship; while the only vessels to be seen other than those were a line of barges propelled by oars following in the wake of the President's, and a few sloops of small tonnage. The contrast marked the progress of the United States in population, wealth, prosperity, and influence among the nations of the earth.*

An elaborate march up Wall Street followed the President's and Vice President's landing. The march, which included delegations from most of the states and territories, ended with a formal reception (for four thousand guests) at the Lawyers' Club in the Equitable Building. The dignitaries enjoyed a banquet at the Lawyers' Club— one for the President and one for the governors of the states—and then took part in a second march to City Hall. After this reception, the President, Vice President, and Governor Hill were given some time off until the Centennial Ball, which took place that evening at the Metropolitan Opera

House and attracted over seven thousand guests—and made a sizeable profit.

On April 30, 1889, the focus of the celebrations, the formal events began with a commemorative religious service at St. Paul's Chapel, the church where Washington worshipped following his inauguration and the only building in lower Manhattan surviving from the 1780s. To mark the occasion, a bronze tablet was commissioned by the Committee of Citizens; it was unveiled on Sunday, December 7, 1890.

Next came "the Literary Exercises at the Sub-Treasury"—the name then used for what we know today as Federal Hall National Memorial. These exercises began with a formal prayer, continued with the Oration of the Day, delivered by the noted speaker Chauncey M. Depew, and concluded with brief remarks by the President and a closing prayer. A special platform was constructed over the steps of the building to accommodate the speakers and invited guests; looming over the platform was the commanding statue of George Washington by John Quincy Adams Ward which had been erected in 1883. Crowds of spectators extended down Broad, Wall, and Nassau Streets. (There was no attempt to re-enact the swearing-in of George Washington on this occasion.)

Following these exercises, the President and other dignitaries were taken to a reviewing stand at Madison Square to review the Grand Military Parade, which proceeded from Wall Street up to Fifty-Ninth Street and Fifth Avenue. This parade was actually the first of two parades—a last-minute solution by the Committee to the problem of having too many groups and individuals

The Centennial of Washington's Inauguration, 1889: President Benjamin Harrison and Vice President Levi P. Morton being rowed to the foot of Wall Street during the Naval Parade, April 29, 1889. Photograph courtesy of the New York City Commission on the Bicentennial of the Constitution.

The Banquet at the Lawyers' Club, Equitable Building, New York City, April 29, 1889. Photograph courtesy of the New York City Commission on the Bicentennial of the Constitution.

The Grand Centennial Ball at the Metropolitan Opera House. Drawing by John Durkin for Frank Leslie's Illustrated Newspaper, May 11, 1889.

who wanted to take part in the parade. The Centennial history estimated that 49,861 men took part in the Military Parade—"the largest body of troops ever brought together in this country in time of peace." The ranks of the parade included thirty governors; 1,168 soldiers from the U.S. Army; 394 U.S. Marines; 1,131 sailors of the U.S. Navy; 288 cadets from the U.S. Military Academy at West Point; 37,794 men from the various detachments of the states' National Guard, state military units, and volunteer militia; 11,876 "Comrades of the Grand Army of the Republic of the United States"—noncommissioned Civil War veterans; and 200 "Companions of the Military Order of the Loyal Legion of the United States"—Civil War veterans who had been commissioned officers of the U.S. Army. The march moved at the rate of "seven thousand troops per hour" without difficulty or incident:

> While the parade was in progress, communication was maintained throughout all its parts by telegraph.... The pageant of April 30th...demonstrated to the world the effectiveness of the citizen soldiery of the United States and the ease and rapidity with which fifty thousand men could be mobilized at any given point...

On the evening of April 30, two thousand singers from forty-five German singing societies performed for a crowd of 50,000 people at Madison Square. The evening concluded with a formal banquet for 800 guests at the Metropolitan Opera House, and with a spectacular display of fireworks by the Unexcelled Fireworks Company at twelve sites throughout Manhattan. "Not a single accident, not a premature explosion, marred the success of the fireworks exhibition."

President Benjamin Harrison delivering remarks at the Literary Exercises for the centennial of Washington's inauguration April 30, 1889.
Photograph courtesy of the New York City Commission on the Bicentennial of the Constitution.

Centennial Ribbon worn by New York City School children.

Former Presidents Rutherford B. Hayes and Grover Cleveland riding to the grandstand to review the Grand Military Parade, April 30, 1889. Cleveland is clearly visible, seated in the coach; Hayes is obscured by the coachman's elbow. Photograph courtesy of the New York City Commission on the Bicentennial of the Constitution.

The Grand military parade—included regular U.S. Army units, detachments from the Navy and Marine Corps, regiments of the National Guard from every state, and veterans' units. It was the single largest assemblage to that date of men under arms in the United States in time of peace. This drawing by T. de Thulstrup for Harper's Weekly, May 11, 1989 illustrates the West Point Cadets passing the reviewing stand at Madison Square Park.

View at Fifth Avenue and 23rd Street, photograph by George T. Bagoe. The temporary arch at 23rd Street was built to resemble a fortress, with turrets and battlements. Decorating the huge span were medallions, busts, and life-size statues of Revolutionary heroes, including the focus of the celebration—George Washington.

On May 1, the second parade—the Civic and Industrial Parade—stepped off from Fifty-Ninth Street and Fifth Avenue and continued down to Canal Street and Broadway. This parade, which the official Centennial history described as "a pageant of peace, which exhibited the progress of a century in the industrial arts," was dominated by groups of recent immigrants, working people, and other ordinary citizens notably different from the Committee of Citizens and their guests. The historian of the Centennial commented: "[E]very trade, every art, every nation, and every representative body of men contributed its brightest and best to make the civic parade an honor to the city of New York. The parade was arranged in ten divisions, each commanded by a "marshal." Among the organizations and institutions represented were: Columbia College, the College of the City of New York, the Hebrew Benevolent and Orphan Asylum, the Bartholdi Battalion of Grammar School No. 15 of Brooklyn, the Knights of Temperance, the Knights of Pythias, the City's volunteer firemen, the New York Fire Department, the New York Police Department, the Tammany Society, the Manhattan Ship Joiners, the Operative Plasterers' Society, the Brooklyn Plumbers' and Gasfitters' Union, the Carpenters and Joiners of America, the United Italian Societies, various organizations representing German-American citizens and Irish-American citizens, the United Polish Societies, and the Colored Centennial Committee. This event concluded the formal commemoration of the Centennial. The November 1889 report of the Finance Committee indicated that the celebration retained a positive balance of $4,741.09.

Photograph of the scaffolding on the permanent arch at Washington Square, 1892. The temporary arch at Washington Square, built for the parades on April 30 and May 1, proved so popular that the Centennial Committee decided to raise funds to create a permanent version. The arch, designed by the noted architect Stanford White, was completed in 1895. Photography courtesy of the New York Historical Society.

The lasting monument of the Centennial is Washington Square Arch. Several temporary wooden arches had been built along the parade route for the Centennial commemoration. The one in Washington Square Park at the foot of Fifth Avenue was so admired that a permanent version was proposed at a formal meeting of the Centennial Committee on Art and Exhibition on May 2, 1889. Ground was broken on April 30, 1890, one year to the day after the Centennial. By May 30, 1890, when the cornerstone was laid, subscriptions for funds to complete the arch amounted to $83,000. By July 24, 1891, subscriptions had reached $106,021.26, with a balance of $9,978.84 needed to complete the arch. The arch was completed in 1895.

In retrospect, the commemoration of the centennial was remarkably characteristic of its time. The prosperous members of the Committee of Citizens and their favored guests saw George Washington almost as one of their own —a wealthy businessman-politician virtually indistinguishable from Andrew Carnegie, Cornelius Vanderbilt, or J.P. Morgan. The centennial was also the occasion for an outpouring of patriotic fervor and Washington idolatry, but these celebrations, largely the work of recent immigrants eager to demonstrate the depths of their patriotism by showing their love for their adopted country's principal national hero, were at best tolerated by those in charge of the formal program. Thus, the commemoration of the centennial reflected the divided state of American society in the Gilded Age as much as it did the general veneration of George Washington and the American experiment in government.

1939: The Forgotten Guest at the Sesquicentennial

By 1939, the sesquicentennial of Washington's inauguration, the first President had become so encrusted with patriotic mythology that he had lost all trace of humanity in the public mind. Indeed, in the 1930s both the American Communist Party and the pro-Nazi German-American Bund claimed Washington as a hero and progenitor. The ease with which extremist groups at both ends of the political spectrum could invoke the spirit of George Washington is further evidence that Washington's general reputation in the minds of the American people carried almost no human or substantive content.

As the nation struggled with the Great Depression, a series of Washington and national historical anniversaries overwhelmed the American people. The celebrating actually began in late 1931, when Republican President Herbert Hoover named the tireless Representative Sol Bloom (Democrat–New York) chairman of the George Washington Bicentennial Commission. For the next seven years, Bloom presided over a series of patriotic commemorations, beginning with the two hundredth anniversary of the birth of George Washington in 1932 and continuing through the sesquicentennial of the framing and adoption of the Constitution to the sesquicentennial of Washington's inauguration. Bloom's patriotic boosterism did not end with the work of the George Washington Bicentennial Commission; when President Franklin D. Roosevelt named a commission to commemorate the 150th anniversary of the Constitution, he designated Bloom as its chairman. Bloom smoothly made the

George Washington Bridge, photograph by Berenice Abbott, 1936. Dedicated a few months before the bicentennial of Washington's birth in 1932, the bridge forged a link between New York and New Jersey and between twentieth-century technology and an eighteenth-century hero.

transition, recycling Washington prints, pamphlet biographies, and other ephemera from the 200th anniversary of the great man's birth for use during the 150th anniversary of the Constitution.

For nearly a decade, the American people were overwhelmed with sheet music, prints, posters, souvenir hatchets and hatchet medals (derived from Mason Locke "Parson" Weems's fable of Washington and the cherry tree), commemorative stamps and coins (including the quarter, whose portrait of Washington is the most durable legacy of Bloom's patriotic campaigning), and pocket Constitutions. The blitz of celebrations, re-enactments, merchandising, and pageantry was designed, in part, to revive American national pride and patriotism in the face of the worst economic slump in American history.

By the 150th anniversary of the first Presidential inauguration, however, the hoopla had exhausted the people's attention and patience. Bloom's commission issued an atlas of Washington's April 1789 journey from Mount Vernon to New York City and sponsored events re-enacting that journey—but drew little attention. The inauguration of Washington was re-enacted on April 30 at Federal Hall National Memorial on a damp, gloomy Sunday morning before dignitaries led by New York's Governor Herbert Lehman and a small, listless crowd.

That same day, President Franklin D. Roosevelt journeyed to New York City to open the principal event of the sesquicentennial, the 1939 New York World's Fair. However, the Fair made only token gestures to its supposed reason for being. The fair's organizers instead emphasized the theme "The World of Tomorrow." James Earle Fraser's sixty-foot plaster statue of George Washington towered over the fairgrounds at Flushing Meadow—but the fair's artistic and architectural advisers decried the decision, preferring to emphasize the twin futuristic symbols of the fair, the Trylon and the Perisphere. A small building sponsored by the Sons of the Revolution, "Washington Hall," displayed the Messmore Kendall collection of Washington memorabilia —but it was relegated to the outskirts of the fairgrounds at Flushing Meadow. The first President was more the ghost at the feast than the guest of honor.

Examples of sheet music by John Philip Sousa and George M. Cohan. In 1932 there were "official" Bicentennial marches, songs, posters, radio broadcasts, and regular news releases.

James Earle Fraser, George Washington. Photograph of statue by Richard Wurts. This sixty-five foot plaster statue dominated Constitution Mall at the fairgrounds. Fraser is most famous for his design of the Indian-head nickel.

Re-enactment of Washington's arrival at Federal Hall; the setting is the world's largest revolving stage, at the 1939 New York World's Fair.

New York World's Fair 1939. Water color by E.P. Chrystie 1887-1960. This painting is similar to an official poster used by the fair.

"The Living Constitution," one of two posters created by the New York City Commission on the Bicentennial of the Constitution. The Commission distributed 75,000 posters to schools, colleges, universities, government agencies, offices and post offices to publicize exhibits, public lectures, and commemorative events throughout New York City during 1987.

3

Organization and Preliminary Activities, 1987-1988

THE New York City Commission on the Bicentennial of the Constitution began its work in early 1987. The Commission had a twofold mandate: (1) to prepare its own projects and to co-ordinate and publicize the programs of other institutions for commemorating the bicentennial of the framing and adoption of the Constitution, and (2) to organize the commemoration, in April 1989, of the bicentennial of the inauguration of George Washington and of the launching of government under the Constitution. This chapter recounts the activities of the Commission in 1987 and 1988; the balance of this book examines the framing and implementation of its plans for the 1989 commemorations.

ORGANIZATION

The City Commission eventually comprised 59 members, appointed by Mayor Edward I. Koch and drawn from the educational, legal, political, business, media, and cultural communities of New York City. Its chairman, Joseph H. Flom, Esq., was a senior partner of the New York law firm of Skadden, Arps, Slate, Meagher & Flom and a recognized leader of the New York bar. Peter S. Kohlmann, Assistant to the Mayor, was appointed Executive Director of the Commission.

In consultation with the Chairman, the Executive Director asembled a staff to carry out the mandate of the Commission and its 1987-1988 programs: Richard B. Bernstein, Historian; Elizabeth T. Farrell, Office Manager; and Roni Schwartz, Program Coordinator. Ellen L. Shapiro of Skadden, Arps served as the Commission's secretary in 1987 and most of 1988; she was succeeded by Alexandra Swift, and then by Mary Weir, also of Skadden, Arps. Joan Stoliar of the Mayor's Commission on Protocol contributed valuable services to the Commission as a graphics designer for several of the Commission's publications.

The Commission expanded its staff as its activities grew in number and variety. For example, in mid-1987, Rachel Conescu, an experienced teacher specializing in history and social studies, joined the Commission's staff as Educational Coordinator. In early 1988, Kathy Madden became Deputy Director; she was succeeded by Michael T. Fiur. With the aid of occasional temporary staff and personnel from other City agencies and departments, the Commission staff worked under the supervision of the Executive Director and in close contact with the Chairman. A list of the Commissioners and staff appears in Appendix A.

THE LIVING CONSTITUTION

The Commission planned its 1987 and 1988 activities and programs with the goal of increasing public awareness of and interest in the origins, history, principles, and continuing relevance of the United States Constitution, as well as New York City's contributions to the making of the Constitution and its subsequent development. (The Commission also hoped that these activities would lay the groundwork with the general public for the Commission's 1989 programs.) As noted in the introduction, the Commission's principal theme was "the living Constitution." It sponsored several publications and programs in 1987 to achieve these goals:

★ Two calendar posters entitled "Celebrate the Living Constitution in New York City." These posters set forth information concerning exhibitions in cultural institutions and

Memorabilia from the bicentennial events included pins commemorating the bicentennial of the Constitution, and the 200th anniversary of George Washington's inauguration.

The Commission distributed about 350,000 copies of the "Self-Guided Walking Tour," its most popular publication.

This brochure, entitled "What Does the Constitution Mean to Us?," explained the significance of the Constitution and New York City's role in its making. More than 75,000 copies of this brochure were distributed by the Commission, its Freedom Bus program, and through museums and historic sites in New York City.

government buildings, public lecture series and panel discussions, commemorative events, and historic sites throughout New York City during 1987. The Commission distributed about 75,000 posters, free of charge, to schools, colleges, universities, government agencies and offices, banks, and post offices for public display and to individuals. In addition, the Commission produced larger versions of the two posters as advertisements in the New York subway system.

★ A brochure providing a self-guided walking tour of lower Manhattan, "designed to introduce [the reader] to the sites...associated with the remarkable history of the Constitution's origins." This free brochure, distributed to individuals requesting it and through such institutions as Trinity Church, The New York Public Library, and The New York Historical Society, was supplemented by a series of historic markers posted at the listed sites. The "Self-Guided Walking Tour" was the Commission's most popular publication. To date, about 350,000 copies have been distributed, both through museums and historic sites throughout New York City and by mail in response to thousands of requests not only from all neighborhoods of New York City but from practically every state and region of the United States.

★ A free brochure entitled "What Does the Constitution Mean to Us?", which set forth capsule explanations of the significance of the Constitution, its origins and principles, and New York City's role in its making. More than 75,000 copies of this "campaign brochure for the Constitution" were distributed by the Commission, by its Freedom Bus programs, and through museums and historic sites in New York City.

★ A series of eight public-service advertisements for display in the New York City mass transit system, with the theme "What the Constitution means to me," presenting brief explanations of basic constitutional principles by New Yorkers from all walks of life. For example, in one poster U.S. District Judge Constance Baker Motley described the importance of the federal courts in the constitutional system; in another, Rabbi Jacob Bronner discussed and praised the Constitution's protection of religious freedom and separation of church and state; in a third, Police Officer Robert Ortiz explained the Constitution's protection of individual rights in the criminal justice system. It is estimated that millions of New Yorkers saw these advertisements while using the city's subways and buses.

FREEDOM BUS

The concept of the Freedom Bus was derived from the 1940s Freedom Train. It was a converted New York Police Department vehicle which carried a portable exhibit entitled "New York City and the Constitution: Where the Experiment Began," a videocassette player and television monitor, and pocket Constitutions (purchased from the federal Commission on the Bicentennial of the Constitution) and City Commission literature. The exhibit, co-curated by Richard B. Bernstein and Roni Schwartz, presented photo-reproductions of portraits of leading New Yorkers who contributed to the making or development of the Constitution (for example, Alexander Hamilton, John Jay, Charles Evans Hughes,

Harlan Fiske Stone, and Judge Amalya Kearse of the U.S. Court of Appeals for the Second Circut), and pictorial explanations of key constitutional principles such as separation of powers, federalism, and individual rights. The video equipment was used to present such programming as: a selection of reports from the PBS series "Moyers: Reports from Philadelphia;" a 12-minute video entitled "Where the Experiment Began: New York City and the Constitution", co-produced by the Commission and WNYC-TV and narrated by Mayor Koch; and other educational video programs. During the summer of 1987, the Freedom Bus visited numerous street fairs and other sites where the general public congregated to display the exhibit, distribute literature, and present the videos.

During September and October, 1987, Roni Schwartz, the administrative co-ordinator, and Rachel Conescu, the educational co-ordinator, revised the Freedom Bus program to concentrate on visits to New York City public schools—including elementary, junior high, and high schools. The revamped program visited thirty schools, presenting a half-day program on the Constitution and its history. As they noted in their July 1988 final report to the Commission,

> *given its small scale, the Freedom Bus School Program was an enormous success. Each of the...schools welcomed [it] because it offered a novel break in the school schedule; more importantly, it provided an array of educational materials otherwise unavailable to New York City public schools.*

In the fall and winter of 1987 and the spring of 1988, Roni Schwartz and Rachel Conescu further revised and expanded the Freedom Bus program, based on their experience the previous

Millions of New Yorkers saw these public service advertisements displayed throughout the city's mass transit system.

What the Constitution means to me...

EVERY day I have to deal with people who might have broken the law. But we don't throw folks in jail only on a cop's say-so. We have some basic rules of fairness in this country. For example, someone is presumed innocent until proven guilty in a court of law. When we gather evidence we have to go by the book. We can't force people to testify against themselves. These rules are established by the Constitution. I do my job as fairly and honestly as I can—but these safeguards protect us all. *That's what the Constitution means to me.*

ROBERT ORTIZ, POLICE OFFICER

THIS ADVERTISEMENT PROVIDED AS A PUBLIC SERVICE OF THE NEW YORK CITY COMMISSION ON THE BICENTENNIAL OF THE CONSTITUTION, EDWARD I. KOCH, MAYOR; JOSEPH H. FLOM, CHAIRMAN; 52 CHAMBERS STREET, NEW YORK, NY 10007.

What the Constitution means to me...

ONE of the things I try to do in this classroom is to train my students to be good citizens. I teach them to respect each other, to honor each other's rights, and to understand and obey laws and rules. But I also teach them to think for themselves, to inform themselves about issues affecting their lives, to have the courage of their convictions, and to stand up for their rights and the rights of others. When they become adults I hope that they will remember these ideas and make them part of their lives. *That's what the Constitution means to me.*

MARGARET SCHULTZ, TEACHER

THIS ADVERTISEMENT PROVIDED AS A PUBLIC SERVICE OF THE NEW YORK CITY COMMISSION ON THE BICENTENNIAL OF THE CONSTITUTION, EDWARD I. KOCH, MAYOR; JOSEPH H. FLOM, CHAIRMAN; 52 CHAMBERS STREET, NEW YORK, NY 10007.

What the Constitution means to me...

IN this country, the Constitution says we can follow any religion or even no religion—as long as we don't hurt other people. I don't have to be a member of a special religion to vote, hold government office, sit on a jury, own a home, or anything. My religion is my own business—not the government's business. And that's important—especially when you believe different things from what most people believe. Freedom to follow my conscience in choosing and practicing my religion—*that's what the Constitution means to me.*

RABBI JACOB BRONNER

THIS ADVERTISEMENT PROVIDED AS A PUBLIC SERVICE OF THE NEW YORK CITY COMMISSION ON THE BICENTENNIAL OF THE CONSTITUTION, EDWARD I. KOCH, MAYOR; JOSEPH H. FLOM, CHAIRMAN; 52 CHAMBERS STREET, NEW YORK, NY 10007.

What the Constitution means to me...

I'M a United States district judge. That would not have been possible even fifty years ago. But it is possible today, and I remember that progress every day that I preside over this court—and I remember how far we still have to go. My job is to decide cases arising under the Constitution and laws of the United States. This means that I regularly must interpret and apply constitutional provisions such as the Equal Protection Clause of the Fourteenth Amendment, which guarantees equal rights to *all* our citizens. *That's what the Constitution means to me.*

CONSTANCE BAKER MOTLEY, SENIOR JUDGE, UNITED STATES DISTRICT COURT

THIS ADVERTISEMENT PROVIDED AS A PUBLIC SERVICE OF THE NEW YORK CITY COMMISSION ON THE BICENTENNIAL OF THE CONSTITUTION, EDWARD I. KOCH, MAYOR; JOSEPH H. FLOM, CHAIRMAN; 52 CHAMBERS STREET, NEW YORK, NY 10007.

Modeled after the 1940s Freedom Train, the Freedom Bus (a converted New York Police Department vehicle) carried a portable exhibit entitled "New York City and the Constitution: Where the Experiment Began."

"Preambles," which became a popular supplement to school curricula on U.S. and New York history, included programs entitled "New York Revisited: A Bicentennial Journey," and "The Constitution Today: Ideas in Action." Photographs courtesy of the New York City Commission on the Bicentennial of the Constitution.

fall. The program they developed, known as "Preambles," expanded each school visit to a full day. They also developed program themes and a more varied array of educational techniques and strategies for presenting them. Finally, they sought to provide teachers with "a number of resource, curricular, and display materials that would reinforce the program themes and bolster the existing curriculum." The units developed for "Preambles" were:

★ "New York Revisited: A Bicentennial Journey," for junior-high-school audiences, focused on New York City and other American cities two centuries ago; this program also taught students that documents, artifacts, and pictorial evidence teach us about the everyday world of the eighteenth century.
★ "The Constitution Today: Ideas in Action," for high-school audiences, emphasized basic principles of constitutional government (federalism, separation of powers, checks and balances, and limited government) and methods of changing the Constitution.

"Preambles" became a much-sought-after supplement to school curricula on U.S. and New York history, social studies, and the Constitution. The program visited 38 junior high schools and high schools, plus five special education sites (including a program for pregnant teenagers and a program for teenagers seeking to overcome drug and alcohol addiction) throughout the New York City school system. The Freedom Bus visited between three and five schools per week, rotating week to week from the junior high school to the high school program. At the conclusion of the program, with the assistance of a generous grant from the New York State Commission on the Bicentennial of the U.S. Constitution, the "Preambles" program purchased resource materials for each of the 38 schools visited during its tour; the junior high schools received "Tavern in a Box," a kit containing slides, artifact reproductions, games, and assignments focusing on the world of the 18th century, and the high schools received the 6-part PBS documentary "Eyes on the Prize." The City Commission donated all the other equipment on the Freedom Bus and materials from the "Preambles" program to the Museum for American Constitutional Government at Federal Hall.

The co-ordinators of the "Preambles" program summed up their experience in their July 1988 final report to the Commission:

Preambles reached over 13,000 students, teachers, and administrators. It inspired each individual on its staff. The tour was an odyssey through the New York City public school system. No two schools were alike. Yet each school repeatedly shattered the illusion—shared by thousands of New Yorkers—that the City's public schools are uniform crypts of violence. To the contrary, the staff found the schools to be filled with concerned administrators, devoted teachers, and bright, energetic students who appreciated its efforts and hope to remain in touch. Their enthusiasm was the richest reward of all.

Where The Experiment Began

The Commission joined with WNYC-TV to produce a half-hour television documentary entitled "Where the Experiment Began: New York City and the Constitution." Written, directed, and co-produced by Chris Pelzer of WNYC-TV, the documentary was narrated by Mayor Koch and featured interviews with historians (including Commissioners Richard B. Morris and Elizabeth P. McCaughey and Commission historian Richard B. Bernstein) and film of portraits, prints, and documents from exhibitions mounted by The New York Public Library and The New York Historical Society. The documentary was aired on WNYC-TV, Channel 31 (UHF), on the night of September 17, 1987, and several times thereafter. (A 12-minute version of this documentary was prepared for use on the Freedom Bus.)

1988: Re-Ratification Convention

In the spring of 1988, the City Commission took part in a program of the New York State Commission on the Bicentennial of the U.S. Constitution to commemorate the bicentennial of New York's ratification of the Constitution on July 26, 1788. Led by Chief Judge Sol Wachtler of the New York State Court of Appeals, the N.Y. State Commission held a "re-ratification convention" in Poughkeepsie, New York (the scene of the original ratifying convention of 1788), to bring together representatives from all over New York State to discuss enduring constitutional issues and problems and to make recommendations for resolution of such issues. The N.Y. State Commission divided New York into eleven districts, and asked government leaders in each district to nominate delegates to the re-ratification convention. Each district held a "town meeting" to discuss what issues its delegates should emphasize in their participation in the Poughkeepsie convention. The New York City town meeting, held in June at Norman Thomas High School in Manhattan, was presided over by Hon. Charles Ramos, Acting Justice of the New York State Supreme Court and a member of the City Commission. The delegates attended the re-ratification convention in Poughkeepsie on July 25-26, 1988.

Part Two

Preliminary drawings of the proposed events for the April 1989 celebration conceived by Radio City Music Hall Productions Inc.

4

Preparing for the Bicentennial

THE commemoration of the bicentennial of the inauguration of George Washington was the ultimate goal of the City Commission. Chairman Flom and the City Commission's staff regarded the marking of this anniversary not only as appropriate in and of itself; they recognized that the history of previous anniversaries of the inauguration (as described in Chapter II) made the marking of its bicentennial a civic responsibility.

PLANNING AND CO-ORDINATION

With the approach of the anniversary, the City Commission hired more staff to deal with day-to-day problems of administration, coordination, and implementation of its programs. Stephanie Adler of the Mayor's Office of Special Projects and Events became Associate Director of the Commission. Other staff members are listed in Appendix A.

The Commission retained Radio City Music Hall Productions, Inc., as producer of the three major events for the April 1989 bicentennial: the Fireworks Spectacular, the Commemorative Inaugural Ceremony at Federal Hall and the Bicentennial Procession. During the preliminary negotiations and in the actual preparations for the bicentennial, both organizations faced the problem of striking a balance between historical accuracy and substantive content, on the one hand, and entertainment of the audience, on the other hand. The shared goal of the Commission and of Radio City in planning for 1989 was to adapt the best features of the earlier major commemorations, in 1839, 1889, and 1939, as well as the events of the first Presidential inauguration in 1789. Barnett Lipton of Radio City, who produced the commemorative events, explained his and his colleagues' underlying thinking: While preserving the spirit of earlier commemorations and seeking to respect the historical record, the bicentennial celebrations reinterpreted the principal features of these commemorations in terms appropriate to 1989.

In planning for the events of 1989, the Commission worked closely with many other government agencies, including the Office of the President; the U.S. Secret Service; the United States Senate and the United States House of Representatives; the Defense Department and the U.S. Army, Navy, and Coast Guard; the national Commission on the Bicentennial of the Constitution chaired by former Chief Justice Warren E. Burger; and several state bicentennial commissions, in particular the New York State Commission on the Bicentennial, chaired by Chief Judge Wachtler and administered by Executive Director Dr. Stephen L. Schechter, and the New Jersey Commission on the Bicentennial, headed by Lynn Edwards and Linda McTigue.

Also, early in its planning, the City Commission determined that a major event on New York Harbor should be a key part of the 1989 celebration, as was the case during the 1889 Centennial. The 1989 Presidential Flotilla and Fleet Week Second Annual Parade of Ships (described in Chapter VII) was the product of extensive and detailed negotiations between representatives of the City Commission and the groups and government departments charged with planning Fleet Week '89.

Ms. Adler, the City Commission's Associate Director, was the principal liaison to the City's Inter-Agency Task Force, which gathered representatives of more than two dozen federal, state, and City agencies and departments in regular meetings to co-ordinate responsibilities for dealing with the logistical problems posed by the celebrations.

The Task Force met weekly for the last six weeks before the events at the end of April. The New York City Police Department under the direction of Deputy Chief Anthony Simonetti assisted tremendously in organizing the many law enforcement and emergency services agencies. During the weekend of April 29-30, the Police Department maintained a 24-hour command center at One Police Plaza with over 40 agencies participating. Throughout the 1989 commemorations, the New York City Police Department, Fire Department, Sanitation Department, Department of Transportation, and Department of Parks and Recreation shouldered the burden of ensuring that the commemorations would be safe and well-organized with the minimum disruption of the regular life of the City.

Mr. Lee Gounardes, of the Community Assistance Unit in the Mayor's Office, oversaw the actions of all City agencies and departments in preparing all public and official viewing areas for all the public events of the bicentennial, including the Presidential Flotilla, the Fireworks Spectacular, the Commemorative Service at St. Paul's Chapel, the Commemorative Inaugural Ceremony at Federal Hall National Memorial, and the Bicentennial Procession.

The complicated task of coordinating and issuing VIP tickets to all the commemorative events was the responsibility of the Mayor's Office of Special Projects and Events. Under the direction of Joan Tucker who was assisted by Barbara Lenefsky, Jackie Friedman and Emily Toll, the office distributed over 8,000 VIP tickets in record time with unusually few problems.

The City Commission also worked with numerous private organizations and institutions, both to publicize their own programs and to implement jointly sponsored events. Details of such partnerships, both formal and informal, appear in Appendix B.

Promoting The Bicentennial
by Michael T. Fiur

Effective promotion of the commemoration of Washington's inauguration was a challenge, primarily because, as noted in the Introduction, it was easier to inspire excitement about the anniversary of a physical structure such as the Statue of Liberty than to celebrate something as abstract as the Constitution and the inauguration of the first President.

Public Relations: With this in mind, the City Commission began its search for public relations counsel early in 1988 to assist with the promotion of the commemorative activities planned for April 29th and 30th. After interviewing nearly a dozen firms, the City Commission selected Hill & Knowlton, the largest public relations firm in the world, to help promote the commemoration. Hill & Knowlton began its work for the City Commission in October 1988. In consultation with the City Commission, Hill & Knowlton deveoped a media strategy for advance publicity for the celebration, leading up to complete coverage of the events.

Imagery: An integral part of promoting the commemoration was the need to develop appropriate imagery—specifically, a logo and a poster image. Ivan Chermayeff of Chermayeff and Geismar Associates agreed not only to design a logo but to donate his creative talents to the City Commission for that purpose. His first version combined the initials "G.W." in large type with the number "200." The City Commission felt that something softer and more evocative of the period was needed. In response, Chermayeff replaced the initials with George Washington's signature. The final logo proved sufficiently versatile that it could be a prominent design element of all City Commission publications, as well as a sought-after logo for other commemorative programs such as those sponsored by the Fraunces Tavern Museum.

The hunt for a design for the official commemorative poster led the City Commission to the School of Visual Arts, which in turn recommended the well-known New York graphic designer Milton Glaser. Like Mr. Chermayeff, Mr. Glaser donated his creative talents to the City Commission. His design presented a portrait of George Washington in profile, composed of multi-colored stars, comets, and meteors suggestive of a fireworks display. The City Commission printed 20,000 24" x 36" copies of this poster, which were distributed to schools, senior citizen centers, post offices, government offices, and other public places throughout New York City. In addition, a much larger version was produced for display in 50 bus-stop shelters throughout the City.

Publicity Efforts: Early publicity efforts included issuing a press release in the fall of 1988 announcing that Republican Presidential nominee George Bush and Democratic Presidential nominee Michael Dukakis had agreed on one thing: they had said that, if elected, they planned to attend the commemoration on April 30, 1989. Meanwhile, Hill & Knowlton worked on "pitching" "long-lead" stories to magazines whose deadlines were fast approaching. While many publications expressed interest in the celebration, their

Milton Glaser, the well-known New York graphic designer, created this official commemorative poster depicting George Washington in profile, composed of multi-colored stars, comets, and meteors suggestive of a fireworks display.

Chermayeff of Chermayeff and mar Associates agreed to design a to help promote the commemorative ts. This logo proved so versatile that ame a prominent design feature of all Commission publications.

stories would not be on the newsstands for five more months.

Working with Hill & Knowlton, the City Commission planned a press conference to announce the plans for the commemoration. A great deal of thought went into selecting the date for this event; after careful review, the conference was scheduled for January 9, 1989. This date was considered to be both close enough to the impending inauguration of George Bush as the 41st President on January 20 to be incorporated into the coverage of the inauguration and far enough in advance so as not to be eclipsed by the inauguration.

Several hundred invited guests, and a handful of reporters, attended the January 9 press conference, which was held at Federal Hall National Memorial at Wall, Broad, and Nassau Streets in lower Manhattan, the site of the 1789 inauguration of George Washington and of the 1889 and 1989 commemorations. Mayor Koch and Chairman Flom each spoke briefly, and Barnett Lipton of Radio City Music Hall Productions outlined the plans for the commemoration. Guests and reporters received press kits containing background materials about the celebration, the City Commission, and George Washington; a schedule of planned events; and a selection of photographs of the 1889 celebration drawn from Bowen's *Centennial History*. The event itself was a success, but press coverage was meager.

Fortunately, President Bush noted several times in his inaugural address that 1989 was the two hundredth anniversary of the first Presidential inauguration and drew links between himself and George Washington; in addition, Mrs. Bush held not only the Bush family Bible but the original Masonic Bible on which Washington had taken the oath of office at Federal Hall. These Presidential invocations of Washington and the first inauguration significantly boosted public awareness of the impending anniversary, but most coverage of Bush's inauguration did not mention the celebrations planned for April 29-30 in New York City.

Not only was the general lack of media attention frustrating; it seemed that the events planned for April were getting far more coverage outside New York than in the host city. One of the greatest obstacles in securing publicity —and, of course, in planning the events themselves—was the White House's refusal to accept formally the Commission's invitation. Although there had been indications that the President would attend, and although Chairman Flom had received a letter on September 30, 1988, indicating then-Vice President Bush's interest in participating, the City Commission staff agreed that this letter was not a firm commitment. Without such confirmation, the news media were reluctant to publicize the events or plan extensive coverage.

The City Commission also hoped to secure the support and participation of the four living former Presidents — Richard Nixon, Gerald R. Ford, Jimmy Carter, and Ronald W. Reagan. Presidents Nixon, Ford, and Carter graciously agreed to permit their names to be used in promoting the events, and were named Honorary Co-Chairmen of the Commission (together with Governor Mario M. Cuomo of New York), but cited various long-standing personal commitments that prevented their actual attendance at the April commemorative events. President Reagan's office never formally responded to the City Commission's invitation to become an Honorary Co-Chairman, and similarly cited long-standing personal commitments that prevented his participation in April. These refusals were deeply disappointing to the City Commission, as many in the news media and the general public had expressed public and private hopes that all living past Presidents would join the current holder of the office on this historic occasion to demonstrate the continuity of the Presidency.

The City Commission had hoped that the weekend of Washington's Birthday would be a good opportunity to raise public awareness of and interest in the April celebrations. (George Washington was born on February 11, 1732, O.S.; the date shifted to February 22 when Great Britain and her American colonies corrected their calendar in 1758. In 1971, Congress shifted the formal commemoration of Washington's Birthday to the third Monday in February, which in 1989 was February 20.) In conjunction with the National Parks Service, the City Commission and Hill & Knowlton set up a photo opportunity at Federal Hall National Memorial: A National Parks Service worker was photographed cleaning the famous John Quincy Adams Ward statue of George Washington on the steps of Federal Hall, dramatizing the efforts to prepare for the April 29-30 celebrations. The photograph was picked up by several newspapers around the country.

By the beginning of April, although some of the "long lead" stories were beginning to appear, there was still very little coverage of the impending events, especially in New York City. Many people began referring to the celebration as "the best kept secret in New York." To remedy this, the City Commission launched an aggressive media campaign and retained additional public relations counsel, Howard J. Rubenstein Associates. Through Rubenstein, the City Commission secured the pro bono services of an advertising agency, Lowe Marschalk; the City Commission paid only for the agency's expenses and the cost of placing the advertisements.

Lowe Marschalk, Rubenstein, and the City Commission developed an advertising plan and created advertisements for newspaper, radio, and cable television. There were two different radio advertisements and two different newspaper advertisements. The first of each pair ran during the week of April 17-23, and the second pair ran during the week of April 24-30. The advertisements were intended to draw crowds to the major public events of the celebration—the Presidential Flotilla and Parade of Ships, the Fireworks Spectacular, and the Bicentennial Procession—and to explain that two other events—the service at St. Paul's Chapel and the ceremony at Federal Hall National Memorial—had limited public access.

About two weeks before the main events on April 30, public attention and the news media began to focus on the commemoration. The White House formally confirmed that President Bush would participate. Moreover, the re-enactment of George Washington's journey from Mount Vernon to New York City (described in Chapter V) began on April 16. As "George Washington" and his party traveled north to New York City, arriving at the South Street Seaport on Sunday, April 23, coverage increased dramatically. (In part, the mishap which crippled "Washington's" coach at Mount Vernon on the 16th increased the news media's interest in the tour, although the rest of the journey took place without incident.)

Other factors which increased public awareness of the impending celebrations were the City Commission's partnerships with WCBS NewsRadio 88 and the New York *Daily News*. The City Commission designated NewsRadio 88 as the official radio station of the bicentennial commemoration, and NewsRadio 88 devoted extensive programming time to public information about the events themselves, the history they were designed to commemorate, and logistical information prepared by City agencies to help people in the New York metropolitan area cope with the events of April 29-30. Similarly, the New York *Daily News* agreed to publish an eight-page supple-

One of the newspaper advertisements developed by the advertising agency, Lowe Marschalk, to help publicize the commemorative events.

THIS WEEKEND, NEW YORKERS WILL CELEBRATE WASHINGTON'S INAUGURATION WITH ALL THE DIGNITY AND DECORUM IT DESERVES.

AND ALL THE FIREWORKS WE CAN GET OUR HANDS ON.

ment that served as a program for the events; drawing on the City Commission's historian, Richard B. Bernstein, for assistance with historical substance. Finally, the *Daily News, El Diario*, the *Staten Island Advance*, WCBS News-Radio 88 and FM station WPLJ Power-95 all held contests for their reading or listening audience, with tickets to the Commemorative Inaugural Ceremony at Federal Hall among the prizes offered. The purpose of these contests was to assure participation by members of the general public in that event.

By the weekend of April 29-30, most New Yorkers were at least aware that events were taking place to commemorate the 200th anniversary of George Washington's inauguration. The many announcements of traffic and parking restrictions by local newspapers and television and radio stations contributed to public awareness. On April 30, according to New York Police Department estimates, approximately one million people lined the route of the Bicentennial Procession up Broadway. Over 300 journalists, representing all major television networks, all New York City television stations, the major local and national radio stations and newspapers, foreign news media, and community newspapers from throughout the city, covered the Commemorative Inaugural Ceremony at Federal Hall.

The commemoration was the lead story on all network evening news programs on April 30. On May 1, the celebration dominated the front pages of almost every newspaper in the nation. Six intense months of planning and hard work had paid off.

Another Lowe Marschalk newspaper advertisement designed for the City Commission, which became part of an aggressive media campaign to increase participation in the upcoming events.

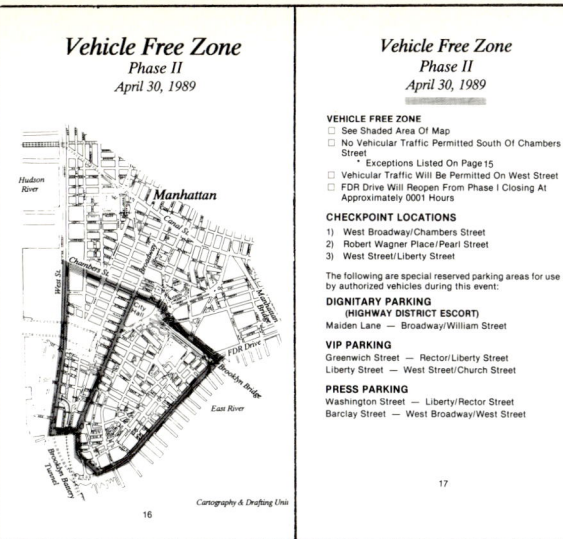

City Commission in conjunction with the Police Department designed these staff passes and parking permits authorizing entrance to restricted areas during the weekend of April 29th and 30th. An information guide, also designed and distributed by the Police Department, contained a map outlining vehicle free zones, V.I.P. and press parking areas, and various checkpoints from which to access the Federal Hall area and the parade route.

FUNDING THE BICENTENNIAL
by Michael T. Fiur

It was just as difficult to raise the necessary funds to support the celebration as it was to promote it. The City Commission developed a budget of $2.3-million. It was decided early on that no City funds would be used to cover production costs. The City provided in kind contribution of two staff positions, office space and telephones and the support of the City agencies. Approximately two-thirds of the budget was devoted to the cost of producing the events, with the other third allocated to publicity/promotion and operations/administration.

Once a budget was in place, the challenge was to raise the funds. Just as the City Commission interviewed prospective public relations counsel, it searched for a marketing and fundraising firm. After meeting with at least six such firms, the City Commission concluded that in-house fundraising would be most efficient and cost-effective. The City Commission retained Jeannine Dowling as a consultant to co-ordinate its fundraising efforts.

As in earlier public celebrations, such as the 1986 centennial of the Statue of Liberty, the City Commission approached sponsors who, in return for their contributions, would receive recognition as sponsors, as well as tickets to various events.

The following sponsorship categories were created:

Presidential Sponsor	$ 250,000
Inaugural Benefactor	$ 100,000
Commemorative Patron	$ 50,000
Bicentennial Patron	$ 25,000
Contributor	$ 10,000

The City Commission began soliciting sponsors in September 1988. The lack of sustained publicity and public awareness made this task even more difficult. By November, the City Commission had only $300,000 in hand, with an additional $200,000 in pledges. Although this was a respectable yield for two months of work, the commemoration was less than six months away, and the City Commission had to determine how much money would be available to finance the events.

Chairman Flom took the lead in seeking the community's support for this project. The process was still a slow one, and it was not until March 1, 1989, that the City Commission had pledges totaling $1-million. This was still only half of the money needed to cover the planned budget. In the middle of April, with two weeks to go, the last of the 46 pledges brought the total sponsorship funds raised to $1.8-million. A list of sponsors appears on page 7.

The balance of the funds needed for the production expenses and operating costs were covered by part of the proceeds of The President's Ball. That function received nearly $1-million more in contributions. After the ball's expenses, the net proceeds of almost $600,000 were divided between an endowment for The Museum of American Constitutional Government (the Commission's permanent legacy for the Bicentennial, described in Chapter IX) and the payment of the City Commission's outstanding production expenses.

The funds for the commemoration were handled by the New York Community Trust/Community Funds, Inc., which acted as the City Commission's collecting and disbursement agent. Herbert West, President; Laurie Slutsky, Executive Vice President; and Sidney S. Whelan, Jr., Vice President/Donor Relations, provided invaluable assistance in managing the account.

The City Commission was also fortunate to have many talented professionals donate their time and skills. Several attorneys assisted the City Commission with the many legal issues inherent in the production of such a large-scale public event: G. Foster Mills, Deputy Chief for Contracts and Real Estate in the Law Department of the City of New York; John F. Breglio and Lawrence Shire, specialists in entertainment law from the New York law firm of Paul, Weiss, Rifkind, Wharton & Garrison; and Bruce Keller and Harry Boadwee, experts in copyright and trademark law with the New York law firm of Debevoise & Plimpton.

George Washington, oil on canvas by Rembrandt Peale, 1823. Known as the "Porthole Portrait," this painting is based on a life study of Washington executed by the 17-year-old Rembrandt Peale in 1795. Painting appeared on cover of invitation shown below. Photograph courtesy of the Mount Vernon Ladies' Association.

The Bicentennial of Washington's Inaugural Journey

Washington's rigorous eight-day inaugural journey from Mount Vernon to New York City will be reenacted from April 16 to April 23, following as closely as possible the route and time schedule the President-elect completed exactly two hundred years ago. Washington and his two traveling companions, David Humphreys and Charles Thomson, will journey through Virginia, the District of Columbia, Maryland, Delaware, Pennsylvania and New Jersey before arriving in Manhattan by barge. As the presidential party passes through a variety of big cities and small towns, Americans will have the opportunity to learn more about the character of George Washington, and once again pay tribute to "The Father of Our Country." The inaugural journey is being sponsored by the Commission on the Bicentennial of the United States Constitution, with the cooperation of state bicentennial committees, the Mount Vernon Ladies' Association, and the United States Army.

To allow a broader participation in this unique bicentennial celebration, the Association has scheduled "George Washington Days at Mount Vernon." From April 17 through April 30, visitors will enjoy daily programs of 18th-century crafts, music, dance, games and military exhibitions, which will provide a glimpse of the world of George Washington on the eve of his presidency.

The culmination of the bicentennial salute to Washington will take place on April 30 at Federal Hall in New York City, where Washington took his oath of office. At exactly 12 noon, Eastern Standard Time, the Association is sponsoring a national bellringing. Churches, synagogues, cathedrals and town halls across America will peal their bells in unison, declaring to an entire nation that Washington is Still First in the Hearts of His Countrymen!

The Regent and Vice Regents
of the
Mount Vernon Ladies' Association
cordially request the pleasure of your company
at a ceremony and reception
to commemorate the
200th Anniversary of George Washington's
Departure from Mount Vernon
for his Inauguration as
First President of the United States
nine-thirty in the morning
Sunday, the sixteenth of April
the Mount Vernon estate

R.s.v.p.
780-2000, Extension 305

Please show this invitation for entry at the Main Gate

The re-enactment of George Washington's departure from Mount Vernon was commemorated on April 16, 1989 by the Mount Vernon Ladies' Association. The Association also presented "George Washington Days at Mount Vernon," a week's worth of programs providing "a glimpse of the world of George Washington on the eve of his presidency." The re-enactment of the arrival in New York City was held at the South Street Seaport on April 23, 1989.

The New York City Commission
on the Bicentennial of the Constitution
Edward I. Koch, *Mayor*
Joseph H. Flom, *Chairman*

The New York State Commission
on the Bicentennial of the Constitution
Mario M. Cuomo, *Governor*
Sol Wachtler, *Chief Judge, Chairman*

The South Street Seaport Museum

in conjunction with

The Federal Commission
on the Bicentennial of the Constitution
Warren E. Burger, *Chief Justice (retired), Chairman*

cordially invite you to attend the

RE-ENACTMENT OF GEORGE WASHINGTON'S
ARRIVAL IN NEW YORK CITY
FOR HIS INAUGURATION AS
FIRST PRESIDENT OF THE UNITED STATES

in celebration of the
Two Hundredth Anniversary
of this historic event

April 23, 1989
at 4:00 p.m.

South Street Seaport
Pier 16

Please respond   (212) 566-4074

5
Recreating Washington's Journey and Arrival in New York City

In July of 1988, Lynn Edwards and Linda McTigue, representing the New Jersey Commission on the Bicentennial, began discussions with the staff of the New York City Commission on the Bicentennial concerning the re-enactment of George Washington's April 16-23, 1789 journey from Mount Vernon to New York City. Ms. Edwards and Ms. McTigue also discussed their proposal with state bicentennial commissions from the other states along Washington's route, and with the national Commission on the Bicentennial. In September 1988, the national Commission hosted a two-day conference at George Washington's plantation, Mount Vernon, to discuss plans for re-enacting the journey. At that time, former Chief Justice Burger expressed his hope that the commemoration of the inauguration in New York City on April 30, 1989 would feature a re-enactment of the original ceremony.

The Mount Vernon conference presented an opportunity for the representatives of the several state and local bicentennial commissions, the Mount Vernon Ladies Association, the national Commission, and the Defense Department's Office for the Bicentennial to discuss the various difficulties that a re-enactment would present. Based on the discussions and suggestions made at the 1988 Mount Vernon Conference, the national Commission set out to co-ordinate a re-enactment of "George Washington's journey to the Presidency," with the several state and local bicentennial commissions assisting in the arrangements as the tour passed through the respective states. John Riley, historian and archivist at the Mount Vernon Ladies Association, provided detailed historical research on the itinerary and events of the tour. Paul Clark, the national Commission's Director of Government Affairs, co-ordinated the journey. The national Commission retained Philadelphia actor William Sommerfield to portray George Washington; Sommerfield stayed at Mount Vernon for the first two weeks of April 1989 to prepare himself for the part and to consult with the staff of Mount Vernon about Washington's character, life, and times.

The re-enactment began on Sunday, April 16, 1989, with "George Washington's" departure from Mount Vernon by carriage. Accompanying Sommerfield were Dr. Herbert Atherton, Deputy Staff Director of the national Commission on the Bicentennial, who portrayed Charles Thomson (the messenger sent by the Confederation Congress to George Washington in 1789), and David C. G. Dutcher, Chief Historian of Independence National Historical Park, who portrayed Colonel David Humphreys, the longtime secretary and aide-de-camp of President-elect Washington. Before a large crowd of journalists and tourists, the carriage began its trip down the semicircular path in front of Mount Vernon. One of the horses, startled by the noise of the crowd and the reporters, left the path and dragged the carriage so that it struck a metal post; the hitch broke off, immobilizing the carriage before it had gone fifty feet. "Washington," "Thomson," and "Humphreys" transferred to a modern van which took them to a spare carriage down the road.

The balance of the journey proceeded without incident and on schedule through Virginia, the District of Columbia, Maryland, Delaware, Pennsylvania, New Jersey, and New York.

The re-enactment of George Washington's departure from Mount Vernon on April 16, 1989, was delayed slightly when one of the horses, startled by the noise of the crowd, left the path in front of Mount Vernon and dragged the carriage into a metal post. The actors portraying Washington, Charles Thomson (the messenger sent by the Confederation Congress to Washington in 1789), and Colonel David Humphreys (Washington's aide-de-camp) were transferred to a spare carriage and continued their journey unhindered.

A crowd of school children gathered to greet "President-elect" Washington, as he made his way from Mount Vernon north and east to New York City.

...tor William Sommerfield, portraying ...orge Washington, stopped at various ...nts throughout the journey, including ...ltimore's Federal Hill and Carroll ...nsion, Philadelphia's Independence ...ll, and visits to Trenton and ...nceton. All along the way onlookers ...ned out to participate in the formalities ...d to wish the "President-elect" well.

PHOTOS COURTESY OF THE U.S. COMMISSION ON THE BICENTENNIAL OF THE CONSTITUTION

"George Washington" departed from Elizabeth, New Jersey on April 23, 1989, a brisk and clear spring day. "Washington" and his party were transported in a shallop (the vessel almost identical to the original barge used in 1789) across New York Harbor. They were welcomed by a crowd of 15,000 well-wishers at South Street Seaport, a few blocks from the site of the original pier at the foot of Wall Street where Washington actually landed.

PHOTOS: LOLA FIUR

The 200th Anniversary
of
George Washington's Inauguration

Re-enactment of George Washington's
Arrival in New York City
For His Inauguration As
The First President of the United States

April 23, 1989
4:00 P.M.

South Street Seaport Museum
Pier 16
Fulton and South Streets
New York City

★ ★ ★

PROGRAM

Performance by the All-City Marching Band
Cannon Salute by the Veteran Corps of Artillery
Answering Salute, HMS ROSE
Arrival & Disembarkation, HMS ROSE
Arrival of George Washington in SHALLOP
Musket Salute by Marine Detachment (1797)
Fife & Drum Procession, Marine Detachment (1797)
Welcoming Remarks
Fife & Drum Procession, Marine Detachment (1797)

Thousands greeted "George Washington" when he spoke after landing at the South Street Seaport on April 23, 1989.

Among other highlights of the tour was its stop at historic Gadsby's Tavern in Alexandria, Virginia; a day-long colonial fair at 200-year-old Montpelier Mansion, near Laurel, Maryland; visits to Baltimore's Federal Hill and Carroll Mansion; a formal welcoming ceremony in Wilmington, Delaware, presided over by Governor Michael Castle; a formal visit to Independence Hall in Philadelphia; visits to Trenton and Princeton, New Jersey; and a re-enactment of the departure ceremony at Elizabeth, New Jersey. Accompanying the "Washington" party was NBC-TV weatherman Willard Scott, who provided color commentary on the journey for the "TODAY" program.

April 23, 1989 was a brisk and clear spring day. Exactly two hundred years after George Washington reached New York City, his arrival was re-enacted at South Street Seaport, only a few blocks from the site of the original pier at the foot of Wall Street where Washington actually landed. "Washington" and his party left Elizabeth, New Jersey, in the *Shallop* (a vessel, provided by Plimoth Plantation, almost identical to the original 47-foot barge used in 1789) which was rowed by cadets from the U.S. Merchant Marine Academy for part of the way and towed by a Coast Guard cutter for the rest of the time. The *Shallop* was escorted by the *"H.M.S. Rose,"* a reconstructed eighteenth-century British gunboat, and by other vessels. "Washington" was met at South Street by Mayor Koch, Chairman Flom, other dignitaries from the City Commission, and an orderly crowd of 10-15,000. The barge's arrival was greeted by cannon fire and musket salutes and a round of three cheers, led by the Mayor. Peter Neill, President, Kathleen Madden, Director of Public Affairs, and the staff of the South Street Seaport Museum coordinated the Seaport's successful management of the April 23 ceremony.

"The Presidency in the 90s" was the subject of a symposium at Fordham University on April 26 and 27, 1989.

6

"The Presidency in the 90's" — The Fordham Symposium

In mid-1988, the Commission approached Professor William J. Small (Larkin Professor of Communications at Fordham University's Graduate School of Business Administration and a former president of CBS News and of UPI), proposing the organizing of a symposium at Fordham on the subject of "The Presidency in the 90's." A series of meetings and discussions among Professor Small, Peter S. Kohlmann and Richard B. Bernstein of the City Commission's staff, Jack David and Steven Finell of the Bicentennial Committee of the Association of the Bar of the City of New York, and Dr. Elizabeth P. McCaughey, a member of the City Commission, produced plans and lists of proposed participants for five sessions. Professor Small extended the formal invitations to the participants and made the necessary logistical arrangements.

The Fordham Symposium was the principal substantive project undertaken by the City Commission. Its cosponsors were Fordham's Graduate School of Business Administration and the New York State Commission on the Bicentennial of the United States Constitution, in association with the Association of the Bar of the City of New York and the Center for the Study of the Presidency. The sessions took place in the afternoon and evening on April 26 and 27, 1989, at the Fordham University Graduate School of Business Administration at the university's Lincoln Center Campus.

The sessions were open to the public and were taped and later broadcast nationally by C-SPAN; edited transcripts of the sessions, the basis of the accounts given below, and video excerpts were prepared by the Fordham University Graduate School of Business Administration and distributed by the City and State Commissions to schools and libraries statewide.

1 The Process of Presidential Selection

MODERATOR: John Chancellor, *NBC News*
Roger Ailes, *Media Advisor*
Ron Brown, *Chairman, Democratic National Committee*
Jeff Greenfield, *ABC News*
Professor Kathleen Hall Jamieson, *University of Texas, Austin*

The panel debated three questions proposed by Professor Small:
   (1) Is the Presidential selection process too long, too expensive, and too discouraging?
   (2) The 1988 campaign was characterized as one of the dirtiest ever. Is this setting a pattern for the 1990s?
   (3) Does the present use of television distort our ability to measure the candidates?

Before beginning his task as moderator, "so you know where I stand," Mr. Chancellor declared his belief that all three questions could be answered *Yes*. Mr. Greenfield challenged this assessment, drawing extensively on the history of Presidential elections to show that the 1988 campaign was neither especially long nor especially dirty, and that television does not distort the process "[c]ompared to the canned speeches that the candidates don't write ...[and] to underground brochures that were distributed throughout all our... history...."

Professor Jamieson focused her response not on the questions themselves, but on the proposals to remedy perceived defects in the Presidential selection process. She insisted that seeking to regulate campaign advertising, or to prohibit it altogether, would give some candidates unfair advantages and remove "the only forum that a candidate has that the candidate controls to put forward the candidate's message." Instead, she suggested a revival of the Fair Campaign Practices Commission, coupled with media coverage of such a commission's findings; in her view, this system would remedy the media's self-perceived burden of objectivity as a bar to critical coverage of misleading campaign tactics. She also urged that the media "abandon the norm that it's only news once" and do extensive and continuing coverage of key issues.

Mr. Ailes pointed out that Presidential politics is "a favorite indoor sport" with the American people, and thus the question whether the campaigns are too long may be beside the point. He also noted that, in a nation where one manufacturer spends $400-million per year to advertise toothpaste, spending $40-million on a Presidential election does not seem excessive. Further, he suggested, "if you look at the whole climate we live in...the garbage that is out there in general," American political campaigns may well be "among the cleanest things on television today." He urged that they also are cleaner and more substantive than campaigns forty and fifty years ago, and argued that the media may contribute to the negative atmosphere of political campaigning more than the candidates or their aides.

Chairman Brown declared that the 1988 campaign may not have been "too dirty, but it was dishonest," noting that both parties' campaigns shared responsibility. He worried that the dishonesty of the campaigns damaged voters' faith in the political process, and thus damaged the process itself:

[I]t is the Presidential election process itself which ought to be that process which encourages participation in our democratic system from the conventions all the way through the primaries and caucuses, all the way through the November election.

That ought to be what motivates and excites people and gets them involved not only in that election but...in their states and local communities. And frankly, it's having just the opposite effect.

The discussion that followed the opening statements focused first on the truth or distortions of campaign advertisements. In the course of the argument, Mr. Greenfield pointed out that "the great virtue of television commercials is [that they give] shorthand bits of information to people who otherwise would know nothing about the campaign at all [a]nd may even encourage them to learn more..."

Mr. Chancellor then asked whether

"The Process of Presidential Selection" was moderated by John Chancellor of NBC News. Participants included Roger Ailes, a Bush Media Advisor; Ron Brown, Chairman, Democratic National Committee; Jeff Greenfield, ABC News; and Professor Kathleen Hall Jamieson, University of Texas, Austin.

the Presidential election process is the best way for the American people to learn which candidate has the skills needed to be a good President. Mr. Greenfield responded that "there is no way to run for President that will measure how good a President you are." Chairman Brown suggested that part of the problem faced by the Democrats in Presidential politics is the lack of a means to "showcase and project Democratic candidates" so that the American people will feel comfortable with them as Presidential prospects. He expressed his hope that the Democratic Party could work to solve this problem in the years ahead.

2 The Presidency and Foreign Policy

MODERATOR: Marvin Kalb,
John F. Kennedy School of Government, Harvard University
Leslie Gelb, *The New York Times*
R. Gordon Hoxie, *President, Center for the Study of the Presidency*
Hon. William P. Rogers,
former Secretary of State (1969-73), Rogers & Wells
Hon. Cyrus R. Vance,
former Secretary of State (1977-80), Simpson Thacher & Bartlett

At the suggestion of Professor Small and Professor Kalb, the panelists discussed three basic issues—first, "the continuing struggle between the White House and the Congress over the control of foreign policy"; second, how the United States will deal in the 1990s with the USSR under Mikhail Gorbachev; and third, "whether the United States ought to shift its emphasis upon foreign affairs from Europe to Asia [and] the Pacific rim."

Dr. Hoxie focused on the first question, citing the profusion of recent proposals for readjusting the constitutional framework of separation of powers and checks and balances to promote efficiency in the conduct of foreign policy. He concluded by endorsing the suggestion of Senator Nancy Landon Kassebaum (Republican-Kansas) that "after all the framers knew what they were putting together...I think there's an awful lot of sense in that...."

Secretary Vance focused on "the international political environment that faces President Bush and the Presidents that will follow him in the 90s." He noted the warming of relations between the United States and the Soviet Union, the slow but real progress made in addressing "dominant security issues," and the emergence of new global issues, including the environment, population, health care, AIDS, and human rights. He suggested that these new issues "may well bring about a realignment of the principal protagonists of the cold war days..." and concluded that the problems of the 1990s will demand "multilateral attention and cooperation in a way that we have not seen practiced in the past."

Secretary Rogers agreed. He based his optimism on the superpowers' recognition of the "terrible consequences that would follow from a nuclear exchange," their realization "that supporting regional conflicts doesn't

work," and the failure of "communism as a form of government and as a substitute for theology."

Mr. Gelb concurred with Secretary Vance and Secretary Rogers, but addressed the question of how the Presidency would respond to the new opportunities and new challenges the other panelists had described. He emphasized the need to reorganize the Presidency "intellectually and bureaucratically" to meet the challenges of the 1990s.

In response to a question from Professor Kalb about the 1973 War Powers Act, Mr. Gelb described it as "a sensible reaction by Congress to an intolerable situation, an intolerable exercise of power on foreign affairs by the President." Secretary Rogers addressed the context out of which the War Powers Act arose—the Vietnam Conflict—and declared, "[T]he greatest mistake that's been made in foreign policy in my lifetime was sending American men and women to fight in Vietnam." Secretary Vance approved of the War Powers Act, suggesting that, "if properly enforced [, it] requires the President to sit back and hear what the Congress has to say, at least the leadership, before the decision is made...." Mr. Gelb argued that, as a practical matter, with or without the War Powers Act, future Presidents will recognize that "it's foolish not to try to consult [Congress] in advance...."

Turning to the question of responding to what Mr. Gelb termed the "Gorbachev revolution," the panelists discussed Mr. Gelb's suggestion for reorganizing the Executive Branch along lines dictated by the problems the nation and the world will face in the 1990s. Dr. Hoxie emphasized the need for a science advisory council, analogous to the National Security Council, and praised the Bush Administration's decision to augment the importance of the President's Assistant for Science and Technology as a step in the right direction.

To conclude the panel, Professor Kalb cited related issues which the panel had not had a chance to address: "We haven't addressed the ways in which we can communicate ideas to the public, if the public itself...is not interested in receiving the ideas in a serious way...." Noting that the press and the media emerge in modern American life as the educators of the American public on political questions, Professor Kalb wondered whether "the press as an institution...[is] responding ...adequately" to the responsibility of educating the public about the new and complex issues the United States will face in the 1990s.

Professor William J. Small organizer of the Symposium on the Presidency in the 90's during the opening session.

3 The Presidency and Public Opir

MODERATOR: Professor William J. Small, *Larkin Professor of Communications, Fordham Graduate School of Business Administration*
David Gergen, *Editor at Large, U.S. News and World Report*
Louis Harris, *Louis Harris Associates, Inc.*
John Seigenthaler, *President, American Society of Newspaper Editors and Chairman/Publisher, Nashville Tennesseean*
Lesley Stahl, *White House Correspondent, CBS News*

Professor Small began by citing the Reagan Administration's conceded fascination with "the public opinion implications of what they were doing" and asked the panel: "[Is] it healthy to have a government so obsessed with public opinion?"

Mr. Gergen conceded that the Reagan White House did pay extensive attention to public opinion polls, "particularly in the early days," but suggested that this concern about public opinion was not new in the White House. He pointed out that Franklin D. Roosevelt was one of the first Presidents to be interested in measuring

public opinion, and that the Agriculture Department's Farm Security Administration studies were among the first public opinion polls. He conceded that more politicians rely more on polls and public opinion surveys now than in the past. As to worrying about the press, Mr. Gergen observed, "if you're in the White House, you feel like you're the obsessee, not the obsessor." He noted the growth of the White House press corps and the media's growing emphasis on the Presidency in American public life. In 1945, Mr. Gergen observed, there were at most only a dozen or so White House correspondents; in 1989, there are 1,700.

Ms. Stahl reminded her colleagues and the audience that President Reagan was obsessed with television and with public opinion, and suggested that the Bush Administration had "taken the pendulum and swung it all the way to the other side of the planet...." She argued that the Presidency has become a "very visceral personal institution" in which the people come to know the President extremely closely and thus react to the President on a visceral level having little to do with substantive policies or issues. She cited a story from her own experience from the 1984 campaign, during which she did a tough story on the campaign and "the White House loved it." Ms. Stahl asked the President's aides, "[D]idn't you hear what I said?" She reported that they didn't care about what she had said, but instead emphasized the "strong and powerful and emotional" pictures that drowned out the intellectual content of her story.

Mr. Harris began by describing the polling that he did for John F. Kennedy's 1960 Presidential campaign; he noted that Kennedy kept the polling confidential and did not even share the results with Robert Kennedy, his campaign manager. He and President Kennedy later discussed the proper role of polling and public opinion in the White House. Kennedy explained that "a President or a head of state in a democracy serves within the jaws of consent of the governed." In making decisions, Kennedy argued, you must decide on the merits of the case. "Then... the proper role of public opinion is [that] you must quickly see if you're within the jaws of consent of the governed." You can be outside that area once, twice, or a few times, but "if you're consistently outside..., you'll soon be permanently out of power.... [I]n effect, public opinion should follow, not lead...."

Mr. Seigenthaler suggested that every President since George Washington has been preoccupied with public opinion, but that "television has made them somewhat obsessed by it." He argued that, in his own way, President Bush is just as concerned with public opinion and the media and just as ready to manipulate public opinion and the media as any of his predecessors.

Professor Small raised the question of international public opinion. "Should a President in the 1990s be more conscious than we've ever seen before in terms of what his words are doing elsewhere?" Mr. Harris agreed, noting that 30 million Europeans speak English fluently and thus have become a new market for English-language news media. Although Presidents have always been aware of the effect of their words and acts overseas, the stakes are greater now than ever before.

Ms. Stahl argued that it was not always good policy just to follow public opinion, pointing out the contradiction between the American people's desire not to pay taxes and the growth of the federal deficit as a key example. Mr. Gergen agreed, drawing on the field of foreign policy to substantiate his argument that "the public is not well informed enough [on foreign policy] to offer a judgment that you ought to follow."

The panel concluded with a discussion of simplification and oversimplification in modern journalism's coverage, during which Mr. Gergen observed, "We just have to understand that for this to be a healthy dialogue, it's important to engage at the level of ideas and serious discussion. And move beyond the personality obsession that we seem to have...."

4 The Presidency and The Financing of Government

MODERATOR: Mike Jensen,
Chief Business Correspondent, NBC News

Dr. Louis Fisher,
Congressional Research Service, Library of Congress; author of Presidential Spending Power (1975)

Alan S. Murray,
Chief Economics Correspondent, Washington Bureau, Wall Street Journal

Peter G. Peterson,
Chairman, The Blackstone Group

Dean Arthur Taylor,
Fordham University Graduate School of Business Administration

Mr. Jensen began this panel by noting, "What we are looking for this afternoon is discussion and not agreement." However, by the end of the session, he ruefully noted that the panelists all agreed on the basic problems facing the Bush Administration and the nation.

Dr. Fisher declared, "If you think back to the last ten years, it seems like we have had nothing but budget questions and spending questions and questions of Presidential leadership or the lack of Presidential leadership." He challenged the many calls for a balanced budget amendment to the Constitution and for an amendment permitting Presidents to exercise "line-item" vetoes over appropriations bills, refuting attempts to draw analogies between state fiscal procedures and policies and those operating at the national level. He also rejected the idea that a line-item veto would generate savings commensurate with the size of the federal yearly budget deficits. He concluded by declaring that, with respect to the subject of the panel, "President Reagan in his eight years in office... [was] by far the most irresponsible President we have had in the budget area," citing the massive growth of the federal deficit during the Reagan Administration.

Mr. Murray predicted that deficits might grow as the nation enters the 1990s to the range of $150-billion to $200-billion per year, and even greater should there be a recession. He predicted that Presidents will find it very difficult to spend money on new programs, that the United States will have to seek foreign partnership in providing funds for such programs as foreign aid and foreign debt relief, and that there will be a rapid growth in "financing programs off the budget." Mr. Murray cited the proposed solution to the savings-and-loan crisis as an example of this last point, deriding the proposal as a "marvelous device."

Mr. Peterson focused on international deficits, including the balance-of-payments deficit. He noted that American overseas borrowing—"$150-billion or more"—amounts to three-and-a-half percent of the gross national product, more than twice the previous record set in the late 1800s. He also noted that the borrowing of the late 1800s was for investment to build up capital in industries and transporation systems such as railroads, whereas the borrowing of the modern period has been for consumption. He suggested that these troubling comparisons should suggest the nature and extent of the financial problems that face the nation. He agreed with Mr. Murray's criticisms of the savings-and-loan proposal, arguing that it "does violence to common sense that really should offend all of us...."

Dean Taylor, noting the "very dismal picture" painted by his colleagues, sought "to say some happy things to you and that's hard to do." Predicting that the world was about to enter "an age of knowledge workers," he argued that the nation had to reconfigure its economy to take advantage of the opportunities the future presented. Not only will the future require the United States to rethink the prevailing assumptions of its economy, but Dean Taylor also saw as necessary "an understanding on the part of our Japanese trading partners that not only they have won but they need to be an expansive and generous winner. That is not happening at the present time...."

Mr. Jensen asked each panelist to make one substantive recommendation to President Bush. Dr. Fisher said, "He'd have to level with the country on what we're doing to ourselves and make it very clear what the dangers are. And then once you do that, then I think you can talk about remedies. And the remedy partly is taxation. But the public is not going to be receptive to taxation unless you explain exactly what it is we're doing to ourselves and our children." Mr. Murray agreed, but pointed out the broad gap between what financial and economics experts see as the major problems facing the nation and what the general public sees as the major problems; the most pressing need, he declared, was to bridge that gap. Mr. Peterson suggested, "Maybe these times call for a President [who] is at least willing to contemplate the possibility of being a one-term President" because the proposals needed to solve the nation's economic problems would of necessity carry with them "major political risks." He suggested, as one example, the readjustment of cost-of-living-allowances downward. He also agreed on the need for more taxes, including gasoline taxes: "the places to [raise taxes] are so obvious that I am stunned that we have any debate about it." Dean Taylor agreed: "George Bush has an opportunity to be part of the problem...[o]r he can be a historic President." He agreed that this would entail the risk of a one-term Presidency but believed that the risk was worth taking. Agreeing with the other panelists about the need for increased taxes, he also stressed the need for retraining: "We need a new kind of industrial worker. An industrial worker [who] has as his or her goal the driving of the cost of raw material and direct labor to zero...."

Dr. Fisher disagreed with the general belief that a President who was willing to take the needed steps to solve the economic crisis would be a one-term President:

I think the country responds well to leadership.... Why not give it a try? Why not have a President tell us the truth for a change? It might be an interesting experiment for us....

What's to prevent Bush from showing the leadership, the education, the interest in ethics, morality? There's nothing holding him back....

I think his greatest danger is to sit in the shadows as he's been doing for three months and do that for another four years. I think he would be defeated because I think he's not going to be as lucky as Reagan was. In his own self-interest, I think he'd better get out in front, face the facts, tell the nation what the facts are, and then point out the things that are fairly obvious, what has to be done....

5 The Future of the Presidency

MODERATOR:
Professor Richard D. Heffner,
Rutgers University—New Brunswick; Moderator, "Open Mind," WNET-TV; Chairman, Motion Pictures Association Rating Commission; Vice Chairman, New York City Commission on the Bicentennial of the Constitution
Professor James MacGregor Burns,
Williams College
Dean John C. Feerick,
Fordham University School of Law
Professor Henry Graff,
Columbia University
Roger Mudd,
MacNeil/Lehrer NewsHour, Washington, D.C.
Theodore C. Sorensen, Esq.,
Special Counsel to President John F. Kennedy (1961-1963); Paul, Weiss, Rifkind, Wharton & Garrison

The issues the last panel confronted were:

(1) Is the Executive Branch, as presently constituted, properly prepared for the decade of the 90's?
(2) How corrupting to the Presidency is the growing concern with public image, particularly because of television?
(3) Can a President function efficiently with a Congress heavily dominated by the opposition party, or is this a healthy check-and-balance?

Dr. Heffner answered these questions, "No; a lot; no," before turning to the panelists.

Professor Burns responded by invoking the theme of the panel and declared that "the future of the Presidency will be much of what we've had, only more so." He pointed out that the Presidency has "a huge accumulation of various types of power and a huge lack of other kinds of power." He identified the deficiencies of power in the Presidency as a lack of planning power, a lack of "integrating power, the inability to pull the government together and really govern," and a lack of "follow-through power, the failure to carry through on the promises that have been made to the people." He also argued that there were serious institutional deficiencies in the Presidency traceable to the constitutional system of checks and balances. He concluded by predicting a serious constitutional crisis, at least as serious as the Watergate crisis, in the years ahead unless the nation made sweeping revisions of the constitutional system.

Dean Feerick pursued the subject of constitutional change as a solution to the problems afflicting the Presidency. He cited the electoral college system of choosing Presidents, and listed some of the potential dangers of that system: (i) the loser of the popular vote can win the Presidency by carrying states with a majority of electoral votes; (ii) if no candidate gets a majority of electoral votes, the House of Representatives has the constitutional responsibility to select a President; (iii) Presidential electors can refuse to be bound by the vote of the people of the respective states when they cast their votes in the electoral college. He declared, "I don't think we ought to wait for a crisis to re-examine and change serious deficiencies in how we select our Presidents." He also suggested that the nation ought to make better use of the ex-Presidents; although the incumbent President should not be impeded by ex-Presidents' activities, ex-Presidents could be of great use in the deliberative processes of government or as senior advisers to the President.

Professor Graff suggested that many of the problems the nation will face in the 1990s will dwarf those who hold the office of President. He also said that, because many problems that used to be handled at state and local levels—"the dreggy problems of society," such as drugs, nuclear waste, and public health—now "arrive on the President's desk," Presidents find their capacity for leadership checked by the need to address these complex, unattractive problems which have no easy solutions. He also agreed with Dean Feerick on the need to re-examine the Presidential selection process, but instead emphasized the problem that most candidates for President are "self-chosen," implying that many who would make excellent Presidents are not considered simply because they do not advance themselves for consideration.

Mr. Mudd began by rejecting the need to assess Presidents based on their first hundred days in office, but addressed himself to the question of "packaging the Presidency." He argued that the nation "was beginning to weary of the televised Presidency, where everything was scripted, where the President stood on the tape on the floor which indicated he was to stand there, where three by five cards replaced papers of state, where nothing was left to chance and where a press conference was a Presidential high wire act...." He also decried the American tendency to praise new Presidents because they were different from their immediate predecessors:

> *We knew Richard Nixon would be great because he was cool and pragmatic and had the plan to get us out of the war that Lyndon Johnson could not disown.*
> *We knew Gerald Ford would be great because he was open and natural in ways Richard Nixon was not.*
> *Jimmy Carter would be great because he was competent and swift and unpolitical in ways that Gerald Ford was not.*
> *Ronald Reagan would be great because he was relaxed and secure and made us proud as Americans in ways Jimmy Carter did not.*
> *And now George Bush will be great because he's not slick and he'll be engaged and immersed and informed and less confrontational in ways Ronald Reagan was not....*
> *What we have done is to bury our Presidents alive under an avalanche of our expectations, and pretty soon the old problems pop through the press releases and the photo ops and the teleprompted speeches and the public begins to notice that life is about the same. The very qualities which made him so attractive when we chose him become the very qualities which make him seem inadequate or out of phase as President....*

Mr. Sorensen warned us not to count on "Providence producing great Presidents," and rejected the belief that Presidents naturally grow into the office. He pointed out that "precedent and institution and gradual evolution" do more to shape a Presidency than the individual talents and abilities of a given President. Finally, although the

Presidency will doubtless change in the years and decades ahead, he doubted that we could predict what those changes would be, and suggested that not all of those changes would be for the good.

Dr. Heffner asked whether Professor Burns was right that a future crisis would be the source of change in the institution of the Presidency. Mr. Sorensen agreed that such a crisis might be on the way—that it "would probably happen in the lifetime of the younger people here." He suggested that it would most likely emerge from the electoral college, as suggested by Dean Feerick:

> When the American people wake up some day after an election and find that the person for whom they voted in a majority is not the President of the United States, there is going to be hell to pay and they won't understand that there's some obscure provision in the Constitution that provides that.

But, Mr. Sorensen added, he disagreed with Professor Burns's suggestion that the Presidency lacked many critical powers.

Professor Burns responded by citing the experience of President John F. Kennedy, whom both he and Mr. Sorensen supported and advised in 1960, and who struggled with Congress for most of his Presidency. "I think if a Jack Kennedy can have the tough time he did in...his Presidency, it was not a very good harbinger of the future, and I think we've seen that played out over and over again, except that other Presidents have sometimes turned to very dubious means. That's why I'm gloomy...about the future of the Presidency."

Dean Feerick commented that, based on the whole two hundred years of the Presidency, perhaps there were not so many reasons for gloom about the future of the institution. He shifted the focus to Congress, wondering whether flaws in the election of members of the House and the Senate, and the excessive power of special interests in Congress, might be equally serious problems for constitutional government in the 1990s and beyond.

Mr. Mudd referred to the presence of television in national politics, arguing that its availability "as a weapon in 20th century government has, in fact, altered the Constitutional balance of powers." Television focuses public attention on the Presidency: "If you go to the Congress, you have 535 funny-looking people all talking at different paces on different subjects. There is no leader." To his regret, bringing television into the House and Senate chambers did not redress the balance. Mr. Mudd warned that "television presents a very dangerous vice in American politics." Presidents must know how to use television, but unless they have the skill to use television, they "will become in the end devoured by television."

Professor Graff spoke of the quality of mystery as an aspect of leadership, and the conflict between the people's desire that their Presidents be extraordinary (which incorporates the idea of mystery) and their desire that their Presidents be ordinary. "You can't have both," he mused—and especially not when television has robbed the Presidency of mystery. Mr. Sorensen agreed, citing the experience of the Nixon White House Tapes as destroying the atmosphere of mystery that hitherto had protected Presidents. "I am simply pointing out that Presidents aren't all that different from the rest of us. But there was some advantage when there was a little more deference because there was a little more mystery...."

★ ★ ★

Professor Small noted in his closing remarks that when Mayor Koch opened the Fordham symposium, he looked over the list of participants and said, "These guys could have *written* the Constitution." The audiences at each of the panels agreed. The discussions were uniformly lively and engaging, and members of the audience took full advantage of the opportunities to ask questions and to continue to talk with the panelists at the conclusion of each session. Public response to the broadcast versions on C-SPAN was equally favorable. In all respects, the Fordham symposium lived up to the hope of its organizers.

7

Saturday, April 29, 1989

THE formal Bicentennial program began on Saturday, April 29, 1989. The two major events of that day invoked New York City's traditions to mark the events of 1789 and the 1889 Centennial.

PRESIDENTIAL FLOTILLA

On a damp and cold morning, the Presidential Flotilla and Second Annual Fleet Week Parade of Ships took place, following the pattern established by the 1889 Centennial. The Parade of Ships, which comprised thirteen U.S. Navy and U.S. Coast Guard vessels (one for each of the original thirteen states), was the centerpiece of the Flotilla, which mustered fifty ships, boats, and other vessels, one for each of today's fifty states. One of these, the Staten Island Ferry, flew instead the flag of New York City from its highest pole. Each yacht flew a flag of one of the fifty states, most of which were sent by state governors in response to requests by Michael Fortenbaugh of the Manhattan Yacht Club. As Commodore of the Flotilla, Mr. Fortenbaugh led the Flotilla in the 93-foot motor yacht *Southern Trail*, the Flotilla's command vessel; he later recalled that, "[d]uring the parade roll call, accomplished by marine radio, each vessel reported [its] position and, with unsolicited embellishment, proudly proclaimed [its] state representation with all of the verbosity usually only found at national political conventions." Hundreds of ships and boats of all types accompanied the Flotilla.

Vice Admiral Howard B. Thorsen, U.S.C.G., welcomed over 3,000 guests to the formal ceremony on Governors Island inaugurating the Flotilla and Parade of Ships. Coast Guard ferries shuttled the guests from lower Manhattan to the island. A V.I.P. reception was held at the Officer's Club on Governor's Island. The official viewing site on the island was chosen so that the Statue of Liberty would serve as a backdrop for the Flotilla. John Reagan "Tex" McCrary of Fleet Week '89 was the master of ceremonies; before the formal program began, the U.S. Coast Guard Band entertained the visitors. Mayor Koch gave the following remarks:

New York began as a city on the water. Verrazano sailed into the bay behind us. Henry Hudson sailed the Half Moon *up the Hudson River. For two centuries after this city was founded in the 1660s, the masts of sailing ships dominated the skyline of colonial New York.*

In 1789, when George Washington arrived in New York City to become the first President of the United States, he was rowed across New York Harbor—an event we saw re-enacted this past Sunday. In 1889, for the centennial of Washington's inauguration, there was a great parade of ships one hundred years ago today. It is particularly appropriate that we begin our Bicentennial weekend celebrations with our own parade of ships. By doing this, we are not only following the great model of the Centennial—we are keeping alive New York City's proud tradition of welcoming ships of all sorts into our harbor on great national anniversaries, and we recall once again that New York is a city whose lifeline is the harbor, and the ocean beyond.

A spectacular event like this one comes about only through the tireless work of many people. On behalf of the people of this City, I want to thank the organizers of Fleet Week '89 for helping to organize this splendid Parade of Ships—the centerpiece of the Presidential Flotilla, now as in the Centennial Naval Procession in 1889—and in particular the U.S. Navy and U.S. Coast Guard. We owe a special vote of thanks to the Coast

JANE L. WECHSLER

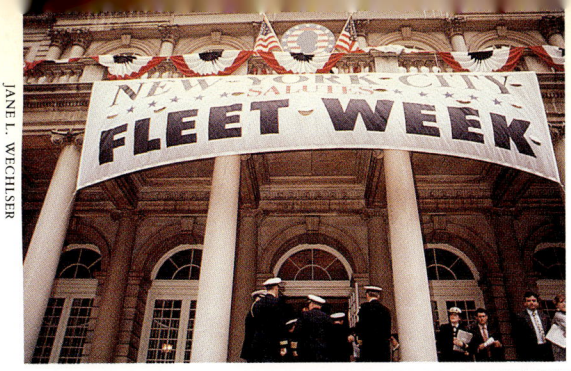

Fleet Week '89 which began with the Parade of Ships on Saturday, April 29, 1989 included many other activities during the week of May 1, 1989.

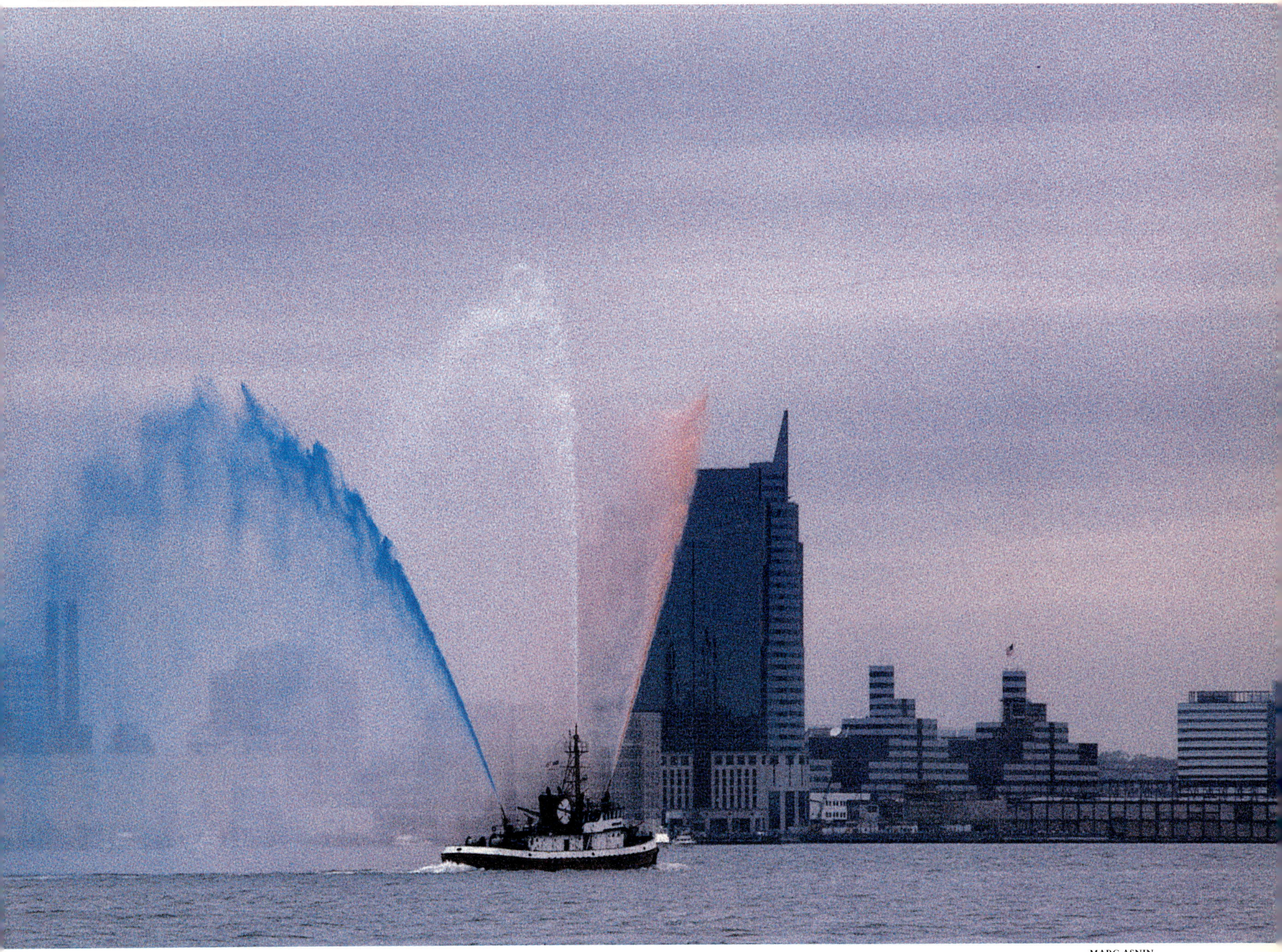

MARC ASNIN

A New York City fireboat celebrated with a spray of red, white and blue water in New York Harbor, as the Presidential Flotilla and Second Annual Fleet Week Parade of Ships began.

Guard for their splendid hospitality here on Governors Island—a perfect place to witness this grand naval procession. And, in recognition of his extraordinary work in organizing the civilian ships, boats, and vessels in the Presidential Flotilla, I want to thank Michael Fortenbaugh of the Manhattan Yacht Club.

One man stands out, and deserves special praise: Zachary Fisher. Zach Fisher's devotion to strengthening the ties between the Navy and New York City have taken many forms. He was the organizing genius behind the Intrepid Sea and Air Museum, and he continues to labor to make that splendid museum one of the glories of this city, as we saw yesterday: Zach was instrumental in arranging for the dedication of the submarine Growler *and the destroyer* Edson *to the Museum's collections.*

Zach is the proud bearer of two honorary titles: He is Honorary Admiral of the Presidential Flotilla, and Honorary Chairman of Fleet Week. Anyone who has worked with him on any of these projects knows that he is far more than an honorary leader.

Two weeks ago, the United States Navy was struck by great tragedy: a sudden, terrible accident aboard the U.S.S. Iowa *that cost the lives of 47 sailors. Every one of us still feels profound sorrow for those who died aboard the* Iowa *and for their families, their friends, and their communities. I want to take this opportunity today to dedicate the Presidential Flotilla, which opens our formal commemoration of the bicentennial of Washington's inauguration, to the memory of the sailors who died on the* Iowa.

Chairman Flom and Honorary Admiral Zachary Fisher, a member of the City Commission, also addressed the guests. Coast Guard and Naval personnel described the vessels comprising the Parade of Ships to the audience at Governors Island. At the other main viewing area, Battery Park, the U.S. Army Band based at Fort Hamilton entertained a crowd of thousands along the shore.

The organizers of the Flotilla and Parade of Ships determined to follow the route of the first Presidential Flotilla from the 1889 Centennial. At 11:30 a.m., the Parade of Ships sailed into New York Harbor through the Narrows, under the Verrazano-Narrows Bridge; when the *Forrestal* reached the Verrazano-Narrows Bridge, it fired a 21-gun salute which was returned by Fort Hamilton in Brooklyn. At the

---

The vessels taking part in the Parade of Ships were (grouped by where they docked after the Flotilla):

MANHATTAN PASSENGER SHIP TERMINAL:
* USS *Forrestal* (CV 59), Captain Louis E. Thomassy, USN *Forrestal*-class aircraft carrier. Home Port: Mayport, FL
* USS *MacDonough* (DDG 39), Commander Arthur D. Cooper, USN *Farragut*-class guided missile destroyer. Home Port: Charleston, SC
* USS *Pharris* (FF 1094), Commander William Busching, USN *Knox*-class frigate. Home Port: Norfolk, VA
* USS *W. S. Sims* (FF 1059), Commander Ira J. Eick, USN *Knox*-class frigate. Home Port: Mayport, FL
* USS *Clark* (FFG 11), Commander Victor H. Ackley, USN *Perry*-class guided missile frigate. Home Port: Philadelphia, PA
* USS *Holland* (AS 32), Captain Frank L. Bowman, USN *Hunley*-class submarine tender. Home Port: Charleston, SC
* USCGC *Hamilton* (WHEC 715), Captain William R. Wilkins, USCG *Hamilton*-class cutter. Home Port: Boston, MA

NAVY PIER, STATEN ISLAND
* USS *Ticonderoga* (CG 47), Captain James M. Arrison III, USN *Ticonderoga*-class missile cruiser. Home Port: Norfolk, VA
* USS *Hayler* (DD 97), Commander Charles E. Mulroy, USN *Spruance*-class destroyer. Home Port: Norfolk, VA

BROOKLYN PIER 6/7
* USS *McCloy* (FF 1038), Lieutenant Commander Joseph A. Benkert, USN *Bronstein*-class frigate. Home Port: Norfolk, VA
* USS *Simpson* (FFG 56), Commander James J. McTigue, USN *Perry*-class guided missile frigate. Home Port: Norfolk, VA
* USS *Fairfax County* (LST 1193), Captain John J. Gallagher, USN *Newport*-class tank landing ship. Home Port: Little Creek, VA

SOUTH STREET SEAPORT, MANHATTAN
* USCGC *Eagle,* Captain David V. Wood, USCG Sailing Barque ("tall ship"). Home Port: New London, CT

same time, the fifty smaller vessels sailed south, down the Hudson River, to welcome the Naval and Coast Guard ships in the Hudson River between the Holland Tunnel and the Battery. The two components of the Flotilla rendezvoused at Governors Island, where the *Forrestal* fired a 17-gun salute returned by the Coast Guard on the island. The full Flotilla then sailed north. Passing Battery Park, the *Forrestal* fired a third, 21-gun salute, returned by the First Veterans Artillery at Battery Park. The Parade of Ships and Flotilla then continued north, up the Hudson River, ending at Piers 90 and 92. The Naval and Coast Guard ships anchored at several points along the shoreline. The vessels remained open to visitors until Thursday, May 4, when they left New York City. The program concluded with flyovers by antique and military aircraft from the Antique Airplane Club of Greater New York.

Vice Admiral Howard B. Thorsen, U.S.C.G. (left), welcomed over 3,000 guests to the formal ceremony on Governors Island. New York City Mayor Ed Koch (center), and City Commission Chairman Joseph H. Flom (right), joined him in viewing the Parade of Ships.

Fleet Week '89 Honorary Chairman Zachary Fisher (above, left) addressing the guests at Governor's Island. Above, is the U.S. Coast Guard ship Eagle as it approaches the Verrazano-Narrows Bridge.

Both Naval, Coast Guard and local vessels joined the Parade of Ships into New York Harbor past the Statue of Liberty and Governors Island. In addition to the thirteen Naval and Coast Guard vessels, the Flotilla mustered fifty ships, boats and other vessels, including the Staten Island Ferry.

Mayor Edward I. Koch conducts the U.S. Coast Guard Band as a parade of U.S. Navy and U.S. Coast Guard ships enter New York Harbor.

Vice Admiral Howard B. Thorsen
on behalf of
The United States Coast Guard
requests the honor of your presence
to view
The Second Annual Fleet Week "Parade of Ships"
and the "Presidential Flotilla"
commemorating the two hundredth anniversary
of George Washington's Inauguration
Governors Island, New York
Saturday, the twenty ninth of April
from ten until one o'clock

R.S.V.P.   (718) 834-2327
               (718) 834-2328

The invitation extended by the United States Coast Guard to view the Parade of Ships from Governors Island.

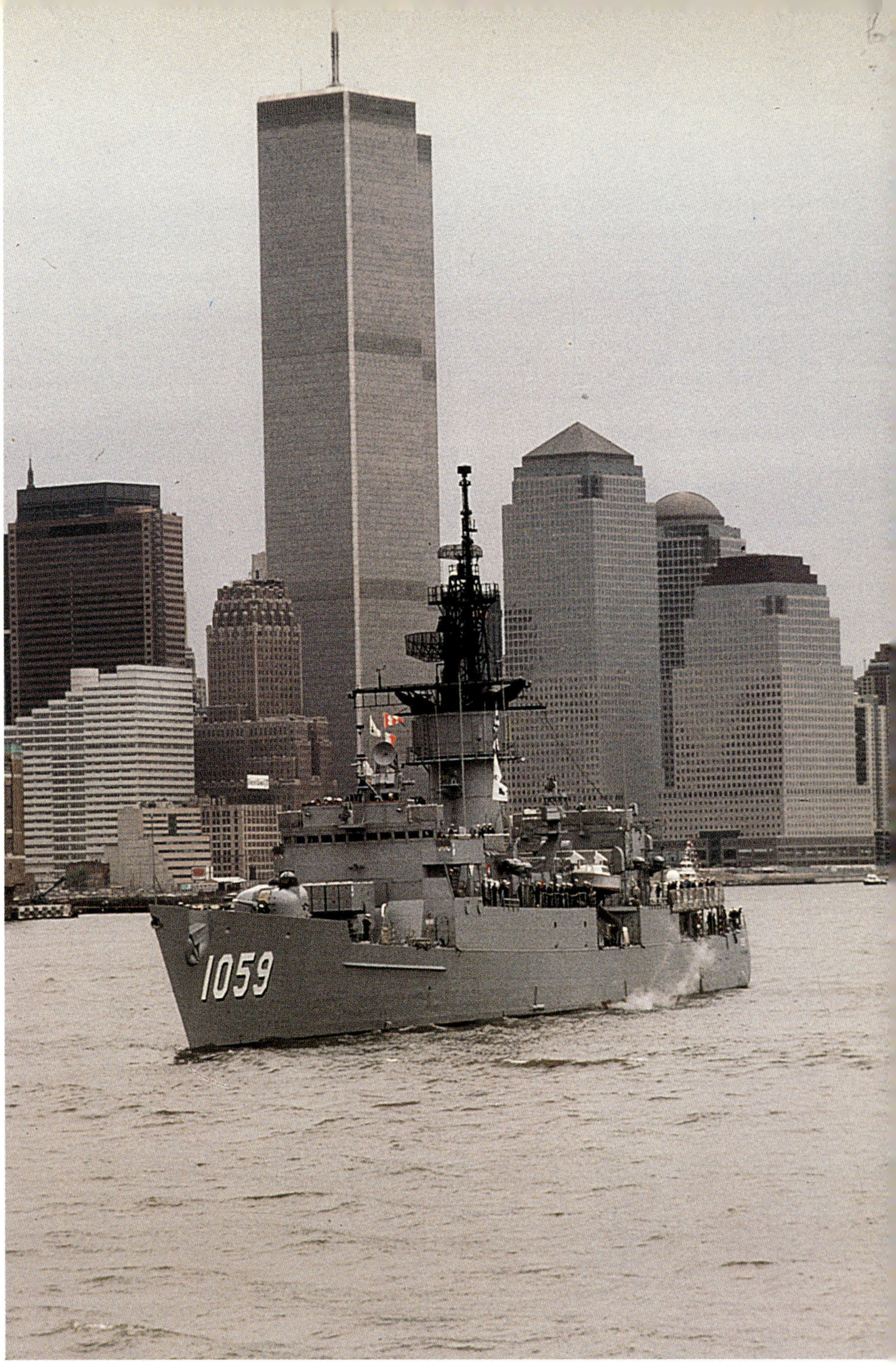

LOLA FUR

JANE L. WECHSLER

JANE L. WECHSLER

Fleet Week ended with a series of activities and celebrations. Shown here are scenes from: dedication of Home Port, presentations on the USS Forrestal, and festivities on the Intrepid Sea, Air, Space Museum.

The chairman of Fleet Week '89 was Gilbert H. Dunham; the honorary chairmen of the event were Joseph L. Dionne, Zachary Fisher, and Richard W. Scheuing. The project director for the event was Terry Dougherty. The City Commission's liaison with the planners of the Flotilla was Stephanie Adler, Associate Director. To honor the captains of the ships participating in the Fleet Week Parade of Ships, Mayor Koch held a special ceremony at City Hall on May 2.

PHOTOS JANE L. WECHSLER

Fireworks Spectacular

Fireworks displays have been a popular New York tradition at least since 1789, when the largest display in the nation's history to that date marked the inauguration of George Washington. New Yorkers have come to expect fireworks as an integral part of public celebrations.

The 1989 Bicentennial of Washington's inauguration reinforced this proud tradition. On Saturday evening, the Grucci Company and Radio City Music Hall Productions, Inc. joined forces to stage a 20-minute "Fireworks Spectacular"—the second-largest in the city's history (the largest being the July 1986 fireworks for the Statue of Liberty). The theme of the display, titled "Hail to the Chief!", was the 200-year history of the Presidency, focusing on Washington, Jefferson, Lincoln, Theodore Roosevelt, Franklin D. Roosevelt, and John F. Kennedy. Former CBS News anchor Walter Cronkite narrated "Hail to the Chief!" from a script prepared by Jeff Ernstoff of Radio City Music Hall Productions, Inc.

Although it was a chilly, drizzly, and overcast evening, the Fireworks Spectacular took place as scheduled, and the weather did not interfere with the success of the display. The low cloud cover was an obstacle for those who chose to watch the fireworks from highrise office buildings in lower Manhattan, but provided a dramatic backdrop for the fireworks for the 500,000 people watching from the streets of Manhattan and Staten Island, at South Street Seaport, or along the Brooklyn shore and on the Brooklyn Heights Promenade.

The Two Hundredth Anniversary of George Washington's Inauguration

The Mayor of the City of New York
Edward I. Koch

and

The New York City Commission
on the Bicentennial of the Constitution
Joseph H. Flom, Chairman

cordially invite you to view the

FIREWORKS SPECTACULAR

in celebration of

The Two Hundredth
Anniversary of
George Washington's Inauguration

April 29, 1989
at 8:30 p.m.

Port Authority Heliport at the East River
and
Pier 11 at Gouverneur Lane

Please respond by April 14
Ticket (indicating location) required
for entry to viewing site

Mayor's Office of
Special Projects & Events
(212) 267-5780

Commemorative invitations and tickets to events of April 29, 1989, included an invitation to the Fireworks Spectacular, and tickets to view the fireworks from various locations throughout the City, one of which was a World Yacht Cruise.

FIREWORKS SPECTACULAR
Saturday, April 29, 1989
THE RIVERANDA
World Yacht Cruises

Boarding: 7:00 p.m. Pier 62
Sailing: 7:30 p.m. West 23rd Street &
Docking: 10:00 p.m. the Hudson River

This ticket is required for boarding and is not transferable

Spectators gathered at many locations throughout New York City to view the fireworks display. Although it was an overcast evening, the weather did not interfere with the success of the display or its popularity with New Yorkers, who have come to expect fireworks as an integral part of public celebrations.

PHOTOS MARC ASNIN

Construction of the V.I.P. dais on the steps of Federal Hall began several days before the actual event. The dais was designed to evoke the appearance of the decorations of Federal Hall National Memorial from the 1889 Centennial as well as the appearance of the original Federal Hall on April 30, 1789.

8

Sunday, April 30, 1989

Two hundred years after George Washington took the oath of office as the first President of the United States, President George Bush, Mayor Koch, Chairman Flom, and many other dignitaries gathered at Federal Hall National Memorial to commemorate the event. By observing the anniversary, the program for the ceremony at Federal Hall declared, "we once again commemorate the success of our durable experiment in constitutional democracy."

COMMEMORATIVE SERVICE AT ST. PAUL'S CHAPEL

St. Paul's Chapel, an Episcopal church located at Broadway and Fulton Street in lower Manhattan, is the oldest public building in the area, and the only structure still standing from the days of the early national period. Built in 1766, St. Paul's is part of the Parish of Trinity Church. In 1789, because Trinity Church had not yet been rebuilt following its destruction by fire during the Revolutionary War, St. Paul's was the principal Episcopal house of worship in New York City. As noted in Chapter I above, George Washington and members of the Senate and House of Representatives attended religious services at St. Paul's following Washington's inauguration on April 30, 1789. In 1889 and again in 1989, therefore, St. Paul's was an integral part of the plans to commemorate George Washington's inauguration. It was especially fortunate that St. Paul's Chapel was newly renovated and restored so that it appears in 1989 as it did in 1789.

Rev. Canon Lloyd S. Casson and Father Percival Ge. Brown of Trinity Parish worked closely with the City Commission staff in planning the service. As almost nothing is known of the original 1789 service except that it included the *Te Deum,* Father Brown, consulting with Phyllis Barr, the historian and archivist of Trinity Parish, prepared a form of religious service drawing on the 1889 commemorative service and the Episcopal Liturgy that would at the same time evoke the events of 1789 and respond to the concerns of 1989. Ms. Barr also curated two exhibitions dealing with the launching of the new national government in 1789 and the part played in the American experiment by leading members of Trinity Parish.

President and Mrs. Bush and their

The City Commission produced commemorative invitations to the events of April 30, 1989. These included entrance tickets to the service at St. Paul's Chapel and to the Federal Hall viewing area.

family were honored guests at the commemorative service, occupying the pew that President George Washington used in 1789 and 1790 when he attended services at St. Paul's. Occupying the Governor's Pew were Governor Mario M. Cuomo of New York, Senators Daniel Patrick Moynihan and Alfonse M. D'Amato of New York, and Mayor Koch. Among the many other dignitaries in attendance were the Spanish and Swedish Ambassadors to the United States, and the British, French, Swedish, Dutch, and Spanish Ambassadors to the United Nations.

The service was ecumenical in the fullest and best sense of the word, with officiants from many of the leading Christian and Jewish denominations in New York City. The service was extensively covered by the news media, in large part because President and Mrs. Bush began their formal participation in the events of the Bicentennial with the commemorative service at St. Paul's. In many respects, the service at St. Paul's was the high point of the bicentennial celebrations, as it was truest to the spirit of the events of 1789.

PHOTOS: JOAN VITALE STRONG

The President and Mrs. Bush and their family occupied the pew that President George Washington used in 1789 when he attended services at St. Paul's Chapel.

Occupying the Governor's Pew were New York Governor Mario M. Cuomo, New York Senators Daniel Patrick Moynihan and Alfonse M. D'Amato, New York Mayor Edward I. Koch, and Chief Judge Sol Wachtler.

Three hundred guests participated in the commemorative service at St. Paul's Chapel, the oldest public building in the downtown Manhattan area.

The Principal participants in the Commemorative Service were The Right Reverend Paul Moore, Jr. Bishop of the Episcopal Diocese of New York, (left) and the Reverend Doctor Daniel Paul Matthews, Rector of the Parish of Trinity Church

Scenes from the Commemorative Service held at St. Paul's Chapel on April 30, 1989.

PHOTOS: JOAN VITALE STRONG

IN CELEBRATION OF THE
TWO HUNDREDTH ANNIVERSARY OF THE
INAUGURATION OF GEORGE WASHINGTON

The illustrations above and on the following pages are reprinted from the Official Prayer Pamphlet used at the Commemorative Service held at St. Paul's Chapel on April 30, 1989. The service was based on similar services conducted at the Chapel in honor of George Washington's Inauguration.

A SERVICE OF
PRAISE AND THANKSGIVING
TO COMMEMORATE THE INAUGURATION OF
GEORGE WASHINGTON
AS FIRST PRESIDENT OF THE UNITED STATES

APRIL 30, 1989
TEN O'CLOCK IN THE MORNING

ST. PAUL'S CHAPEL
BROADWAY & FULTON STREET
IN THE CITY OF NEW YORK

PARTICIPANTS IN THE SERVICE

The Reverend Doctor Daniel Paul Matthews
Rector of the Parish of Trinity Church
Officiant

The Right Reverend Paul Moore, Jr.
Bishop of the Episcopal Diocese of New York

The Reverend Doctor Louis C. Gerstein
Minister Emeritus of Congregation Shearith Israel
First Lector

The Reverend Matthew F. Mulloy
Assistant Pastor of St. Peter's Roman Catholic Church
Second Lector

The Reverend John Wallace Moody
The Parish of Trinity Church
Intercessor for the Country

The Reverend Percival Ge. Brown
The Parish of Trinity Church
Intercessor for the Government

The Reverend Elizabeth A. Sherman
The Parish of Trinity Church
Intercessor for the People

The Reverend Canon Lloyd Stuart Casson
Vicar of Trinity Church and St. Paul's Chapel
Intercessor for the Social Order

Mr. David R. Jette
Verger

The Choir of Trinity Church
Mr. Larry P. King, *Organist and Music Director*
Ms Catherine C. Burrell, *Apprentice in Church Music*

Adam Gilbert, *Recorder*
Dongsok Shin, *Harpsichord*

The People shall stand during the fanfare as the President of the United States of America takes his place at the George Washington pew.

A FORM OF PRAISE AND THANKSGIVING

The People stand as the Clergy enter the chancel.

The Officiant shall begin the Service by reading the following sentences of the Holy Scripture.

Holy, Holy, Holy, is the Lord God Almighty, which was, and is, and is to come!
Revelation 4:8

O give thanks unto the Lord, and call upon his Name; tell the people what things he hath done.
Psalm 105:1

Officiant	O Lord, open thou our lips.
People	**And our mouth shall show forth thy praise.**

Then follows the congregational singing of the Psalm 122

PSALM 122 — *O 'twas a joyful sound*   St. Anne

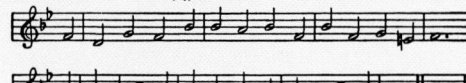

I
O 'twas a joyful sound to hear
our tribes devoutly say,
Up, Israel, to the temple haste,
and keep your festal day.

II
At Salem's courts we must appear
with our assembled pow'rs,
In strong and beauteous order rang'd,
like her united tow'rs.

III
'Tis thither, by divine command,
the tribes of God repair,
Before his ark to celebrate
his name with praise and pray'r.

IV
Tribunals stand erected there,
where equity takes place;
There stand the courts and palaces
of royal David's race.

V
O pray we then for Salem's peace,
for they shall prosp'rous be,
Thou holy city of our God!
who bear true love to thee.

VI
May peace within thy sacred walls
a constant guest be found,
With plenty and prosperity
thy palaces be crown'd.

VII
For my dear brethren's sake, and friends
no less than brethren dear,
I'll pray-May peace in Salem's tow'rs
a constant guest appear!

VIII
But most of all I'll seek thy good
and ever with thee well,
For Sion and the temple's sake,
where God vouchsafes to dwell.

Metrical version by Tate and Brady
William Croft (1678-1727)

THE FIRST LESSON

A reading from the Book of Micah. (Revised Standard Version - M

It shall come to pass in the latter days that the mountain of the h
Lord shall be established as the highest of the mountains, and sha
up above the hills; and peoples shall flow to it, and many nations
and say: "Come, let us go up to the mountain of the Lord, to the h
God of Jacob; that he may teach us his ways and we may walk in his
out of Zion shall go forth the law, and the word of the Lord from Je
shall judge between many peoples, and shall decide for strong nati
and they shall beat their swords into plowshares, and their spears i
hooks; nation shall not lift up sword against nation, neither shall
war any more; but they shall sit every man under his vine and u
tree, and none shall make them afraid; for the mouth of the Lord
spoken. For all the peoples walk each in the name of its god, but we
the name of the Lord our God for ever and ever.

Then shall the Choir sing the anthem.

Te Deum Laudamus in F   Orlan

Sung by The Choir of Tr

THE SECOND LESSON

A reading from the Gospel according to Luke. (RSV - Luke 10:25

And behold, a lawyer stood up to put Jesus to the test, saying
what shall I do to inherit eternal life?" He said to him, "What is
the law? How do you read?" And he answered, "You shall love the Lo
with all your heart, and with all your soul, and with all your st
with all your mind; and your neighbor as yourself." And he said to
have answered right; do this, and you will live." But he, desirin
himself, said to Jesus, "And who is my neighbor?" Jesus replied, "
going down from Jerusalem to Jericho, and he fell among robbers, v
him and beat him, and departed, leaving him half dead. Now by cha
was going down that road; and when he saw him he passed by on th
So likewise a Levite, when he came to the place and saw him, passe
other side. But a Samaritan, as he journeyed, came to where he wa
he saw him, he had compassion, and went to him and bound up
pouring on oil and wine; then he set him on his own beast and bro
an inn, and took care of him. And the next day he took out two dena
them to the innkeeper, saying, 'Take care of him; and whatever mor
I will repay you when I come back.' Which of these three, do you th
neighbor to the man who fell among the robbers?" He said, "The one
mercy on him." And Jesus said to him, "Go and do likewise."

The People sing a hymn of praise to God

The God of Abraham praise — Leoni

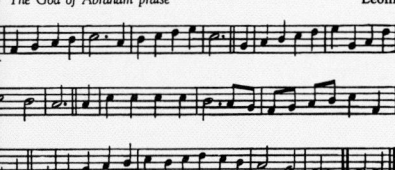

I
The God of Abraham praise, who reigns enthroned above;
   Ancient of everlasting days, and God of love;
the Lord, the great I AM, by earth and heaven confessed:
   we bow and bless the sacred Name for ever blest.
II
He by himself hath sworn: we on his oath depend;
   we shall, on eagle-wings upborne, to heaven ascend:
we shall behold his face, we shall his power adore,
   and sing the wonders of his grace for ever-more.
III
There dwells the Lord, our King, the Lord, our Righteousness,
   triumphant o'er the world and sin, the Prince of Peace;
on Zion's sacred height his kingdom he maintains,
   and, glorious with his saints in light, for ever reigns.
IV
The God who reigns on high the great archangels sing,
   and "Holy, holy, holy," cry, "Almighty King!
Who was, and is, the same, and evermore shall be:
   eternal Father, great I AM, we worship thee."
V
The whole triumphant host give thanks to God on high;
   "Hail, Father, Son, and Holy Ghost" they ever cry;
hail, Abraham's Lord divine! With heaven our songs we raise;
   all might and majesty are thine, and endless praise.

Thomas Olivers (1725-1799), alt.

THE PRAYERS

...o hast given us, thy servants, this good land for our heritage, we
... and give thee humble thanks for these United States of America,
... vast multitudes brought here from many lands.
...thee and thank thee, O God.

...nders of this country, who with confidence in thy providence won
... hemselves and for us, and lit the torch of freedom for nations then

...thee and thank thee, O God.

For the natural majesty and beauty of this land, and the great resources of this nation.
We praise thee and thank thee, O God.

We all do implore thee, O God; so to rule the hearts of thy servants, George, the President of the United States, and all others in authority, that they may do justice, and love mercy, and walk in the ways of truth.
Have mercy on thy servants, O God.

So to guide and bless our Senators and Representatives in Congress, that they may enact such laws as shall be in the welfare of this people.
Have mercy on thy servants, O God.

So to bless the courts of justice and the magistrates in all this land; and give unto them the spirit of wisdom and understanding, that they may discern the truth, and impartially administer the law in the fear of thee alone.
Have mercy on thy servants, O God.

We all do beseech thee to hear us, O God; and that it may please thee to behold and visit the cities of this land, that the ties of mutual regard may be renewed, to the elimination of poverty, prejudice, and oppression, and the prevalence of peace with righteousness, and justice with order.
We beseech thee to hear us, O God.

That it may please thee to bless all who live and work in rural areas with the gift of seasonable weather and a bountiful harvest of the fields, that all the people of our nation may give thanks for food and drink and all other bodily necessities of life, and may respect those who labor to produce them.
We beseech thee to hear us, O God.

That it may please thee to keep us mindful of those who suffer from want and anxiety from lack of work, that we may so use our public and private wealth that all may find suitable and fulfilling employment, and receive just payments for their labor.
We beseech thee to hear us, O God.

O Almighty God, hear us as we pray thee to bless all schools and colleges, that they may be centers for sound learning, new discovery, and the pursuit of wisdom, that all who teach and all who learn may find the truth.
O God, hear our prayers.

Pour out thy healing power upon all who are sick in body, mind, or spirit; graciously comfort those living with AIDS; have compassion upon all who through addiction have lost their health and freedom; and to them that care for them, give patient understanding.
O God, hear our prayer.

Help us, O God, to finish the good work here begun. Strengthen our efforts to blot out ignorance and prejudice, and to abolish poverty and crime. And hasten the day when all our people, with many voices in one united chorus, will glorify thy holy Name. *Amen.*

The Bishop of New York shall say a Prayer of Thanksgiving

O Lord our Governor, whose Name is exalted in all the world: We give you thanks for the innumerable blessings you have bestowed upon all of humankind from the days of old unto this time. Moreover, we render our most heartfelt praise for the chosen vessels of your grace and the lights of the world in their generation. For raising up your servant George Washington, and giving him to be a leader and commander to the people; for granting him victory over kings, and for bestowing upon him many excellent gifts; for inclining the hearts of those in Congress to wise choices, and for granting them vision into the days to come; for a settled Constitution and for just laws; for freedom to do the right and liberty to speak the truth; for the spread of knowledge everywhere among us, and for the preservation of the faith, we bless your holy Name, and humbly beseech thee to accept this our sacrifice of praise and thanksgiving, through Jesus Christ our only Savior and Redeemer. *Amen.*

Then the Bishop shall say the Benediction

The Lord bless thee and keep thee.
The Lord make his face to shine upon thee and be gracious unto thee.
The Lord lift up his countenance upon thee and give thee peace. *Amen.*

The Officiant concludes the service saying

Their sound has gone out into all lands, their message to the ends of the world.
Psalm 19:4

Here endeth the Order of Praise and Thanksgiving

After the singing of the following hymn, the ministers shall leave the chancel.

HYMN - *O beautiful for spacious skies* — Materna

I
O beautiful for spacious skies, for amber waves of grain,
   for purple mountain majesties above the fruited plain!
America! America! God shed his grace on thee,
   and crown thy good with brotherhood from sea to shining sea.
II
O beautiful for heroes proved in liberating strife,
   who more than self their country loved, and mercy more than life!
America! America! God mend thine every flaw,
   confirm thy soul in self-control, thy liberty in law.
III
O beautiful for patriot dream that sees beyond the years
   thine alabaster cities gleam, undimmed by human tears!
America! America! God shed his grace on thee,
   and crown thy good with brotherhood from sea to shining sea.

Katherine Lee Bates (1859-1929), alt.

V.I.P.s were escorted from St. Paul's Chapel to Federal Hall via the "Presidential Tram." Mayor Edward I. Koch and Chief of Staff Diane Coffey (left), and New York Senators Daniel Patrick Moynihan and Alfonse M. D'Amato (below), ride the tram from the front of St. Paul's across Broadway to Federal Hall.

The large video screen set-up next to Federal Hall displays the Commission's logo. The screen was used to provide coverage for those spectators unable to get close enough to see the various speakers and parade participants.

The press section provided newspaper, radio and television reporters an unobstructed view of the President and other V.I.P.s on the Federal Hall dais.

The view of Federal Hall from the spectator seats extending down Broad Street from Wall Street to Exchange Place. Spectators came from all over to be part of this commemorative event.

PHOTOS: MARC ASNIN

President Bush received a silver Tiffany bowl from Mayor Koch commemorating the 200th Anniversary of George Washington's Inauguration. Joining them during the presentation were Peter Valone, Majority Leader of the City Council (far left), and Diane M. Coffey, the Mayor's Chief of Staff.

Mr. Steven J. Ross and Mr. Ronald Pechman (left), benefactors of the bicentennial, pose with the President and Mrs. Bush (center) in the rotunda of Federal Hall. City Commission Chairman Joseph H. Flom (right) looks on.

Mayor Edward I. Koch gives the crowd a "thumbs up" sign as he stands on the dais at Federal Hall.

PHOTOS: JOAN

Federal Hall The Seat of Congress
(Line engraving by Amos Doolittle after Peter LaCour, 1790) Pierre L'Enfant refurbished Federal Hall for Washington's inauguration, adding a large frieze displaying the arms of the United States and, as described by the Columbian Magazine, "Tablets over the windows, filled with thirteen arrows and the olive branch united, [to] mark it as a building set aside for national purposes."
(Courtesy Stokes Collection, New York Public Library)

```
COMMEMORATIVE INAUGURAL CEREMONY
FEDERAL HALL NATIONAL MEMORIAL
APRIL 30, 1989
Prelude
United States Army Band (Pershing's Own)
Institutional Radio Choir of Brooklyn, NY
Entrance of the President of the United States
The Presentation of Colors
Continental Color Guard of the United States, 3rd Infantry (The Old Guard)
National Anthem of the United States of America
United States Army Band (Pershing's Own)
Under the Direction of Col. Eugene W. Allen
Invocation
His Eminence Archbishop Iakovos
Primate of the Greek Orthodox Church of North and South America
Welcoming Remarks
Joseph H. Flom, Chairman
NYC Commission on the Bicentennial of the Constitution
The Honorable Edward I. Koch
Mayor of the City of New York
"My Country 'Tis of Thee"
Institutional Radio Choir
The Bicentennial of Congress
The Honorable Lindy Boggs
Member of Congress, Chairman of the Commission on the Bicentenary
of the U.S. House of Representatives
The Honorable Daniel Patrick Moynihan
United States Senator
A Prayer for the Nation
Most Reverend William J. McCormack, D. D.
National Director, Society for the Propagation of the Faith
Auxiliary Bishop, Archdiocese of New York
A Dramatization of the
Inauguration of George Washington
Warren E. Burger, Chairman
Commission on the Bicentennial of the U.S. Constitution
Chief Justice of the United States, 1969-1986
Introduction of the President of the United States of America
The Honorable Alfonse M. D'Amato
United States Senator
Presidential Address
President George Herbert Walker Bush
Presidential Bicentennial Procession
```

The official program from the Commemorative Inaugural Ceremony at Federal Hall National Memorial included a hand cancelled U.S. Postage Stamp issued in honor of the executive branch of government.

COMMEMORATIVE INAUGURAL CEREMONY AT FEDERAL HALL

Following the service at St. Paul's, the dais guests boarded a "Presidential Tram" which carried them down lower Broadway to Federal Hall National Memorial for the Commemorative Inaugural Ceremony. (A listing of the dais guests appears in Appendix C.) The other invited guests, numbering more than 4,000, passed through special checkpoints staffed by the New York Police Department and the U.S. Secret Service. The seating for these guests extended down Broad Street from Wall Street to Exchange Place.

Working throughout the previous week, carpenters and electricians had constructed a special dais over the steep steps of the Greek Revival structure. The dais was designed to evoke the appearance of the decorations of Federal Hall National Memorial from the 1889 Centennial, as well as the appearance of the original Federal Hall on April 30, 1789. In recognition of some of the more sobering changes in American society in the two centuries since Washington's inauguration, three 8' by 10' panels of bulletproof glass shielded that part of the dais where President and Mrs. Bush were to sit. In order that all the invited guests and those standing in the public viewing areas beyond Exchange Place could see and hear the ceremony, a large television screen was set up in Nassau Street and loudspeakers were aimed along Wall Street and down Broad Street.

The ceremony at Federal Hall began with a musical prelude by the United States Army Band (Pershing's Own) and the Institutional Radio Choir of Brooklyn, New York. At the conclusion of their performance, President and Mrs. Bush joined the guests on the dais built over the steps of Federal Hall National Memorial. The Continental Color Guard of the United States, 3rd Infantry (The Old Guard) presented the colors of the United States and of the branches of the nation's Armed Forces. Following the National Anthem, Archbishop Iakovos, Primate of the Greek Orthodox Church of North and South America, delivered the invocation.

Chairman Flom welcomed President and Mrs. Bush and the other guests gathered for the ceremony, after which Mayor Koch also addressed the crowd. The Institutional Radio Choir then performed "My Country 'Tis of Thee."

Because April 1989 was also the month of the bicentennial of the Congress of the United States, Representative Lindy Boggs (Democrat-Louisiana), Chairman of the Commission on the Bicentenary of the U.S. House of Representatives, and Senator Daniel Patrick Moynihan (Democrat-New York) delivered remarks commemorating the two hundredth anniversary of the First Congress.

The Most Reverend William J. McCormack, D.D., National Director of the Society for the Propagation of the Faith and Auxiliary Bishop of the Archdiocese of New York, then delivered a prayer for the nation.

Former Chief Justice Warren E. Burger, chairman of the national Commission on the Bicentennial of the Constitution, then delivered a brief talk on the events of 1789 and their significance in American history, after which William Sommerfield once more took central stage as "George Washington" in a dramatization of the events of April 30, 1789. When "Washington" arrived in his carriage, the entire crowd of onlookers stood and cheered him. Surrounded by delegates of the Council of the Original Thirteen States in period costume, "Washington" repeated the oath of office after "Chancellor Robert R. Livingston," while "Samuel A. Otis" held the original Masonic Bible on which the real President Washington swore his oath in 1789 and "Charles Thomson" and "David Humphreys" stood by. He then delivered a condensed version of President Washington's original inaugural address. Paralleling the events of two centuries

The George Washington statue on the front steps of Federal Hall.

Actor William Sommerfield portraying George Washington arrives at Federal Hall to take the oath of office.

Demonstrators disrupt the President's remarks to call attention to what they viewed as his lack of attention to the problem of AIDS.

A member of the Institutional Radio Choir, which performed during the commemorative ceremony.

William Sommerfield re-enacts Washington's oath of office surrounded by the delegates of the Council of the Original Thirteen States in period costume.

before, "Washington" was greeted with a roar of musketry and the cheers of the crowd as he prepared to lead the Presidential Bicentennial Procession.

Senator Alfonse M. D'Amato (Republican-New York) then introduced the President of the United States. The high point of the ceremony was the President's remarks (given below in a text provided by the White House):

Two centuries ago, standing here, a man took an oath before a new nation, and the eyes of God. An oath that I, like 40 before me, have since had the privilege to take.

Everyone here today can still feel the pulse of history, the charge and power of that great moment, in the genesis of this Nation.

Here, the first Congress was in session beginning a tradition of representative government that has endured for 200 years. Here, the representatives of 13 colonies struggled to find balance, order, and unity between them. And here, our first President issued a solemn address.

One who was there wrote: "This great Man was agitated and embarrassed, more than ever he was by the leveled Cannon or pointed Musket. He trembled, and several times could scarce make out to read." But who wouldn't have felt some trepidation, undertaking a task which had never been tried in the world's history?

On that day, Washington spoke of his "conflict of emotions." He admitted his "anxieties" and "deficiencies," as honest men will.

But then—as his first official act—he turned to God, fervently, for strength. For he knew that the advancement of America, while it might rely on its Presidents, would surely depend upon Providence.

How unlikely it must have seemed then, that we might become United

States. How uncertain, that a republic could be hewn out of the wilderness of competing interests. How awesome the prospect must have seemed, to the man charged with guiding the new Republic made possible by his leadership in battle.

But George Washington defined and shaped this office. It was Washington's vision—his balance of power and restraint, as he watched over the Constitutional Convention in 1787—that gave the delegates enough confidence to vest powers in a chief executive unparalleled in any freely-elected government, before or since.

It was Washington's vision, his balance, his integrity, that made the presidency possible. The Constitution was, and remains, a majestic document. But it was a blueprint—an outline for democratic government, in need of a master builder to ensure its foundations were strong.

Based on that document, Washington created a living, functioning government. He brought together men of genius—a team of giants, with strong and competing views. He harnessed and directed their energies. And he established a precedent for 40 presidents to follow.

For all of the turmoil and transformation of the last 200 years, there is a great constancy to this office, and this Republic. So much of the vision of that first great President is reflected in the paths pursued by modern Presidents.

Today, we reaffirm ethics, honor, and strength in government. Two centuries ago, in his first inaugural address, Washington spoke of a government "exemplified by all the attributes which can win the affections of its Citizens, and command the respect of the world."

Today, we say that leaders are not elected to quarrel, but to govern. On that spring day in 1789, Washington pledged that "no party animosities will misdirect the comprehensive and equal eye which ought to watch over this great assemblage of communities and interests."

Today, we seek a new engagement in the lives of others—believing that success is not measured by the sum of our possessions, our positions, or our professions, but by the good we do for others. Two hundred years ago today, Washington said there exists "in the economy and course of nature, an indissoluble union between virtue and happiness, between duty and advantage."

Today, we speak of values. At his inauguration, Washington said that "the foundations of our National Policy will be laid in the pure and immutable principles of private morality."

Over the last 200 years, we have moved from the revolution of democracy, to the evolution of peace and prosperity.

But so much remains constant. So much endures.

Our faith in freedom: for individuals, freedom of choice; for nations, self-determination and democracy.

Our belief in fairness: equal standards, equal opportunity; the chance for each of us to achieve, on our own merits, to the very limit of our ambitions and potential.

Our enduring strength: abroad, a strength our allies can count on, and our adversaries must respect; at home, a sense of confidence, of purpose, in carrying forward our nation's work.

My starting point has been a respect for American institutions—for Congress, for the Judiciary, for the executive branch, and for government at all levels—and a firm belief in maintaining the powers of the Presidency.

The Presidency, then as now—in oath, and in office—derives from the strength and the will of the people.

George Washington, residing at Mount Vernon, felt himself summoned by his country—to serve his country. Not to reign—not to rule—but to serve.

It was the noblest of impulses—because democracy brought a new definition of nobility. It means that a complete life, whether in the 18th or 20th Century, must involve service to others. Today, just as Washington heard the voice of his country calling him to public service, a new generation must heed that summons.

More must heed that call.

Today we stand—free Americans—citizens in an experiment of freedom that has brought sustained and unprecedented progress, and blessings in abundance.

As we dedicate a museum of American Constitutional Government, let us together re-dedicate ourselves to the principles to which Washington gave voice, 200 years ago.

Let our motivation derive from the strength and character of our forefathers—from the blood of those who have died for freedom—and from the promise of the future that posterity deserves.

Let us commit ourselves to the renewal of strong, united, representative government, in these United States of America.

★ ★ ★

As the President began to speak, a group of six demonstrators from the organization ACT UP began chanting slogans to draw attention to the problem of AIDS and to denounce the President for what the demonstrators viewed as his failure to act. The President continued speaking, but several members of the audience confronted the demonstrators. At this point, police officers restored order and removed the demonstrators without incident.

President Bush and Mayor Koch share a laugh as Archbishop Iakovos, Primate of the Greek Orthodox Church of North and South America stands by.

Former Chief Justice Warren E. Burger, chairman of the National Commission on the Bicentennial of the Constitution, focused his remarks on the events of 1789 and their significance in American history.

Senator Daniel Patrick Moynihan addressed the audience to commemorate the bicentennial of the First Congress.

President Bush shakes Senator Alfonse M. D'Amato's hand after being introduced by him.

The view from the dais. President Bush addresses the audience which extends for many blocks down Broad Street. The dais is protected by bullet-proof shield.

PHOTOS JOAN VITALE STRONG

When the President concluded his remarks, a shower of confetti fell on the dais and the crowd. At that moment, the sun finally broke through the clouds, adding to the bright, festive air of the celebration. The President and his entourage then boarded the Presidential limousine and led the Bicentennial Parade up Broadway.

BICENTENNIAL PROCESSION

The Bicentennial Procession was planned in the grand tradition of the two great parades of the 1889 Centennial. Comprising both military and civilian units, the procession began at the corner of Wall and Nassau Streets, headed up Wall Street past Federal Hall National Memorial to Broadway, then turned north up Broadway to Waverly Place, where it circled Washington Square Park before disbanding there. Beginning shortly after noon, the parade ended about 3:00 p.m. More than one million people stood along lower Broadway to watch the parade and cheer the 10,000 marchers. The order of the parade appears on page 111, taken from the official program distributed at Federal Hall National Memorial.

In the financial district alone, more than 5,000 police officers and scores of U.S. Secret Service agents filled the area to direct traffic, watch over the dignitaries, and assist the orderly crowd of onlookers. After the parade, over 400 sanitation workers, operating 57 mechanical brooms, 70 collection trucks, 78 haulster-type vehicles, one open-body truck, and 13 street flushers removed more than 340 tons of litter and refuse from the parade route at a total cost of $150,000.

At the conclusion of President Bush's remarks, the sun finally broke through the clouds, brightening what had until then been a cloudy day. At that moment, a shower of confetti fell on the dais and on the crowd, and it was clear that the celebration had begun.

MARC ASNIN

WILLIAM H. MARTIN

MARC ASNIN

Scenes from the conclusion of The Commemorative Inaugural Ceremony at Federal Hall, April 30, 1989.

MARC ASNIN

The parade progressed up Broadway, led by "George Washington" in his carriage, followed by Mayor Koch and the 10,000 marchers.

PHOTOS: MARC ASNIN

PHOTOS: MARC ASNIN

Presidential descendants join in the parade. Including, in carriage below, Lacey Washington, George Washington's great-great-great-great-great niece (rear), and John Washington, Jr., a descendant (right) during the Presidential Procession.

"George Washington" and his entourage arrive at Washington Square Park, where celebrations are already underway.

PRESIDENTIAL BICENTENNIAL PROCESSION

Division I
Old Guard Fife & Drum Corps *(Washington, D.C.)*
Commander-in-Chief's Guard *(Washington, D.C.)*
"George Washington" *(Portrayed by William Sommerfield)*

Division II
United States Army Commander of Troops
United States Military Academy Band *(West Point, NY)*
United States Military Academy Corps of Cadets *(West Point, NY)*
Third United States Infantry, "The Old Guard" *(Fort Myer, VA)*
United States Army Colors
United States Army National Guard, The 1st Battalion 258th Field Artillery
(Fort Tilden, NY)
United States Army Reserve, 5th Battalion 5th Field Artillery *(Ft. Totten, NY)*
United States Marine Corps Commander of Troops
United States Marine Band *(Washington, D.C.)*
The United States Marine Corps From Marine Barracks, 8th and I *(Washington, D.C.)*
United States Marine Corps Colors
United States Navy Commander of Troops
The United States Navy Band *(Washington, D.C.)*
United States Naval Academy Midshipmen *(Annapolis, MD)*
United States Navy Colors
United States Navy Ceremonial Guard *(Washington, D.C.)*
United States Naval Reserve
(Ft. Schuyler The Bronx, Staten Island, Brooklyn and Amityville, NY)
United States Air Force Commander of Troops
The United States Air Force Band *(Washington, D.C.)*
United States Air Force Academy Cadets *(Colorado Springs, CO)*
United States Air Force Honor Guard *(Washington, D.C.)*
United States Air Force Colors
United States Air National Guard 106th Aerospace Rescue & Rocovery Group
(Westhampton Beach, NY)
United States Air Force Reserve 512th and 514th Military Airlift Wing
(McGuire Air Force Base, NJ and Dover Air Force Base, DE)
United States Coast Guard Commander of Troops
The United States Coast Guard Band *(New London, CT)*
United States Coast Guard Academy Cadets *(New London, CT)*
United States Coast Guard Colors
United States Coast Guard Ceremonial Guard *(Washington, D.C.)*
United States Coast Guard Reserve Group *(New York, NY)*
United States Merchant Marine Academy Band *(Kings Point, NY)*
United States Merchant Marine Academy Cadets *(Kings Point, NY)*

Division III
Veteran Corps of Artillery *(New York, NY)*
Patriots of Northern Virginia *(Arlington, VA)*
New York Ancients Fife & Drum Corps *(Mt. Vernon, NY)*
Lexington Minutemen *(Lexington, MA)*
Ancient Mariners Fife & Drum Corps *(Westbrook, CT)*
Brigade of the American Revolution *(Plainfield, NJ)*
Minutemen of Long Island *(Huntington, NY)*
Huntington Militia *(Huntington, NY)*
Colonial Musketeers of Hackettstown *(Hackettstown, NJ)*
Living History Association *(Arden, NY)*
C.A. Palmer Fife & Drum Corps *(Palmyra, NY)*
Essex Sailing Masters *(Essex, CT)*
Artillery Company of Newport *(Newport, RI)*
New Jersey Colonial Militia Fife & Drum Corps *(Morristown, NJ)*
Germantown Ancients Fife & Drum Corps *(Danbury, CT)*
Sons of the Revolution *(New York, NY)*
Daughters of the Revolution *(New York, NY)*
Children of the Revolution *(New York, NY)*

Division IV
WCBS-AM NewsRadio 88 *(New York, NY)*
New York Police Department Emerald Society Band *(New York, NY)*
New York Police Department Academy Cadets *(New York, NY)*
New York Police Department Mounted Police *(New York, NY)*
Honorary Grand Marshal Helen Hayes
Westchester Brassmen Drum & Bugle Corps *(Harrison, NY)*
Ebony Horsewomen Association *(Hartford, CT)*
Antique Farm Wagon and Fiddlers *(North Bergen, NJ)*
Black Rodeo Champion Cowboys *(New York, NY)*
Antique Wells Fargo Stage Coach *(North Bergen, NJ)*
Mother Cabrini High School Band *(New York, NY)*
Suburban-ettes Baton Twirlers *(Chelmsford, MA)*
National Dance Institute *(New York, NY)*
All-City High School Marching Band *(New York, NY)*
La Salle Military Academy Drill Team *(Oakdale, NY)*
Portraits of the Presidents *(Carried by the La Salle Military Cadets)*
Descendants of the Presidents
Valley Stream High School Streamers Drill Team *(Valley Stream, NY)*
Tottenville High School Band *(Staten Island, NY)*
George Plimpton *(in carriage)*
Butler High School Sequinettes Drill Team *(Butler, PA)*
Seaford High School Marching Band *(Seaford, NY)*
Hebrew Orphans Asylum *(New York, NY)*
Long Lake Gals Kazoo Band *(Long Lake, NY)*
German-American Tricentennial Bikers *(Philadelphia, PA)*
New York Fire Department Emerald Society Band *(New York, NY)*
Totally Confident Drill Team *(Los Angeles, CA and New York, NY)*
Princeton University Marching Band *(Princeton, NJ)*
International Sidesaddle Association *(Mt. Holly, NJ)*
Judd Hirsch *(in carriage)*
Bond Street Theatre Stiltwalkers *(New York, NY)*
National Foundation to Protect the American Eagle *(Nashville, TN)*
George Washington High School Band *(Philadelphia, PA)*
Fame Fire Company Antique Pumper *(West Chester, PA)*
Horsedrawn Antique Ice Wagon *(North Bergen, NJ)*
New York Police Department Horsedrawn Wagon *(New York, NY)*
Sasha Nanus' 1890's Street Performers *(Nw York, NY)*
Horsedrawn Antique Dairy Wagon *(North Bergen, NJ)*
Cardinal Spellman High School Marching Band *(Bronx, NY)*
The Wheelmen Antique Bicycles *(Glenolden, PA)*
New York Times Antique Carriage *(North Bergen, NJ)*
Heinz Company Horsedrawn Wagon *(Pittsburgh, PA)*
Pennsylvania Briefcase Brigade *(Philadelphia, PA)*
Big Apple Corps Band *(New York, NY)*
Tyler Quarter Horses *(Newark, DE)*
DeWitt Clinton High School JROTC *(Bronx, NY)*
First Company Governor's Footguard *(Hartford, CT)*
"You're A Grand Old Flag"

Presidential Descendants
by Peter Nissen

One of the more interesting events organized by the City Commission took place early on Sunday morning, April 30, when lineal and collateral descendants of each of the Presidents of the United States made their way into downtown Manhattan, converging at Fraunces Tavern. This historic establishment, founded in 1762 by Samuel Fraunces, is almost as old as George Washington himself; he dined regularly there and, in December 1783, he bade farewell to his officers at a dinner marking the end of the Revolutionary War.

The first to arrive—a full hour early—was Captain Horatio A. Lincoln, a former destroyer captain from the Second World War, with his son Robert, daughter Susan, and son-in-law David Brown. They had traveled from California. Mrs. Hilles Morris Timpson (Van Buren), financier Theodore Roosevelt IV, stockbroker David Roosevelt, and the Washingtons arrived. Andrew Jackson VI, lawyer, and his wife Janet arrived, having traveled from Knoxville, Tennessee; it was their first visit to New York. Once there was a quorum, the press took a group photograph.

At 10:30 a.m., author and singer Margaret Truman arrived, completing the occasion: Descendants and relatives of every President in the 200 years of the office—forty Presidents in all—were assembled in one place for the first time. From Lacey Washington, the first President's great-great-great-great-great-great niece, to Karen Dennis, President Reagan's third cousin, the full history of the institution was represented. Their ages ranged from 9 to 82.

The descendants traded family stories and talked of politics and history. Helen Marie Taylor had a bone to pick with Milbry Polk. As *The New York Times* reported it the next day, Mrs. Taylor had learned that President Polk was tardy in dispatching aid to Zachary Taylor, then a general fighting in the Mexican War. "I want to ask them why he was so slow," she demanded. In one corner, Captain Lincoln was talking with Eleanor Sayre, Woodrow Wilson's granddaughter. "Yours was a Democrat, and mine was a Republican," said Captain Lincoln. "But," Mrs. Sayre replied, "he was a *liberal* Republican."

An unexpected descendant was John Washington, Jr., a 27-year-old actor from Los Angeles, who flew into New York to surprise his family, who were our Washington representatives. The Washingtons were the favorites of the press. Not only were they the family of the day—they were also very photogenic and knew how to handle media attention.

Many of the descendants already knew one another: the Nixons and Carters, for example, and the Virginia families—the Tylers, Norfleets (Fillmore), Valentines (Madison), Washingtons, and Taylors. Clement E. Conger (Washington), Curator Emeritus of the White House, and Eleanor Sayre (Wilson), a curator at the Boston Museum of Fine Arts, knew one another professionally. In fact, some discovered new cousins among descendants of other Presidents.

It is actually not unusual to find such relationships. Genealogist Gary Boyd Roberts has shown, in his book *Ancestors of American Presidents* (Carl Boyer, 1989), how President Bush is related to fifteen other Presidents within ninth-cousin range. In fact, he and George Washington are ninth cousins, seven times removed. Mrs. Bush, *nee* Barbara Pierce, is a fourth cousin, five times removed, of President Franklin Pierce. A combination of geography, politics, and the small radius of Washington society—especially before the twentieth century—has created inevitable convergences and coincidences among the ranks of Presidential descendants and relatives. The best recent example is the marriage between David Eisenhower and Julie Nixon. Eliza Garfield, our "triple descendant," is directly descended from William Henry Harrison, James A. Garfield, and Benjamin Harrison. Harrison Ruffin Tyler, John Tyler's grandson, is also related to William Henry Harrison, the President whose death made Tyler President. The descendants signed a scroll that declared their "trust in the endurance and success of the American system of constitutional government." The scroll was the dedicatory instrument of The Museum of American Constitutional Government at Federal Hall National Memorial, the City Commission's permanent legacy, "charged with teaching our children and grandchildren the arts, history and wisdom of freedom." That morning, 39 signatures were set down, representing 40 Presidents (Grover Cleveland Amen's one signature counted for two Presidencies, for his grandfather was both the 22nd and 24th President). The scroll was later sent to the White House, signed by President Bush (the 41st President), and installed at the Museum of American Constitutional Government in New York.

The descendants walked *en masse* to their seats at the Commemorative Inaugural Ceremony at Federal Hall National Memorial. During the ceremony, the descendants were acknowledged and cheered.

The centerpiece of the Federal Hall ceremony—for the descendants as well as for everyone else—was the speech by President Bush, who had just completed his hundredth day in office. During President Bush's remarks, as noted earlier, a chant arose from within the reserved section: six demonstrators from the organization ACT UP stood on their chairs, waving signs and chanting, "One hundred days and nothing done—what about AIDS?" The President continued speaking, not acknowledging the protestors. But an infuriated John Washington headed for the demonstrators. He was followed closely by Helen Marie Taylor, who not only shouted back at the demonstrators, but jumped on a chair herself and wrested one of the signs from their hands. New York City police soon calmed both sides and sent them on their ways. The scuffle—a case study of the First Amendment in action—made national news.

Mrs. Taylor, an art collector, actress and former government official, was no novice in catching the attention of the public and the press. She had once lain down in front of bulldozers to protect the historic cobblestones of Richmond, Virginia.

As the ceremony ended in a storm of colorful confetti, the descendants prepared to march in the Bicentennial Procession. Some walked, others rode in carriages. The carriage reserved for the Tylers and the Valentines had lost its hitch due to a wild horse, but an old-time open "paddy wagon" was commandeered to carry them, much to their delight.

The descendants' unit was led by the two blond Hoover children, Margaret and Alexander. William Howard Taft III, 74, walked the whole two-and-one-half miles—no great feat for a man who walks ten miles daily. The Washingtons had their own carriage. Captain Lincoln took the helm—or, rather, the reins—of his carriage, and Chandler Roosevelt, 13, sat next to her driver. Luci Baines Johnson was asked if she was Washington's daughter. "Hell no, I'm LBJ's daughter!" she exclaimed, and spent the rest of the parade working the crowd and telling everyone who she was. The Harding family were favorites, dressed in period clothes and sporting Harding campaign pins. Dr. Harding, president of Harding Hospital in Worthington, Ohio, carried the actual watch and walking-stick that his Presidential great-uncle had used when taking the oath of office in 1921. Lawrene Nixon Anfinson was grateful that the crowd did not disparage her uncle, as others so often do. She discussed this problem with Ulysses Grant Dietz. "He said he gets it all the time," she reported. "We all get it. I was talking to Luci Baines Johnson about it, and she said she gets it too."

The Procession ended in Washington Square, where a reception greeted the descendants. John Washington, Jr. rushed out to get a tuxedo for the ball that night, knocking on the closed doors of a rental shop until he procured one—at 5:00 p.m. on a Sunday.

The black-tie gala was attended by a total of 47 descendants and family members, who held the place of honor: an extended table set in front of the stage. Here, they were toasted by Mayor Koch and greeted by Peter Kohlmann, the Commission's Executive Director. Senator Alfonse D'Amato of New York asked to have a picture taken with John and Angela Works, the Jefferson descendants. The evening ended with perhaps the ultimate expression of bipartisanship: the Carters dancing with the Fords.

★ ★ ★

The process of finding and inviting Presidential descendants began with an excellent resource, *Burke's Presidential Families of the United States* (2nd ed. 1981). From this book's genealogical charts, followed up by extensive conversations with the staffs of Presidential museums, libraries, and historic sites, I was able to get in touch with the closest relatives. Often the people I tried to reach had moved; some were deceased.

Sometimes just finding the Presidential museum was a challenge. In search of Buchanan authorities, I called telephone information for Mercersburg, Pennsylvania, where President Buchanan was born, and asked for the Buchanan Homestead. On the first try, I reached the Buchanan Inn, which asked if I wanted dinner reservations. Then I followed a lead to Buchanan Associates, which specializes in growing hydroponic tomatoes. Finally, I located James Buchanan Henry, a rhythm-and-blues musician from Austin, Texas, through a call to his former residence in New Jersey.

My quest for a Zachary Taylor descendant started with a call to a funeral home in the town where he was buried. The staff of the funeral home referred me to the correct cemetery, whose staff in turn gave me the name of a Taylor relative. President Fillmore was buried in Buffalo, New York; the woman who answered the phone at the cemetery said that Fillmore's grave was "a big drawing card for visitors." She consulted the "transcript of death" for some vital information about descendants. Eventually I reached Robert Fillmore Norfleet III, a senior in high school, where he was on the lacrosse and football teams.

Descendants themselves were helpful in tracking down others. Benjamin Harrison Walker provided names of Harrisons, Adamses, Clevelands, and Garfields, including that of his niece Eliza Garfield. Eliza, who works on educational schooners, spent the summer after our event sailing to Leningrad on a "citizen's diplomatic voyage."

I found Richard Nixon's descendant by a shot in the dark: a Mr. Nixon listed in the Social Register said that he was not related to the President, but suggested that I try author Jessamyn West, a distant Nixon cousin. A call to her publisher produced her address, and finally I was in contact with Nixon relatives. Four referrals later, I reached Ed Nixon, the President's brother, who did not come, but gave us his niece's number—and that of Carter relative Hugh Carter, whom he knew.

A college alumni office was the key to finding Ulysses Grant Dietz, about whom I knew only his age and school. Captain Horatio Lincoln turned up through Ford's Theater in Washington, D.C.; the manager there said, "Some

Lincoln relatives passed through here a few years ago—let me see if I can find their names."

For President Tyler, there was no question whom we would choose, after examining the family tree. Harrison Ruffin Tyler is the grandson of the tenth President. The President, born in 1790, was 63 when he fathered his 13th child, Lyon Tyler. Lyon had his fifth child, Harrison, when he was 75. Harrison and his wife Paynie still live at and run Sherwood Forest, the President's plantation in Virginia.

A week before the bicentennial celebrations, we were still several names short of the required forty. With much persuasion, we won over Robin Lawford (Kennedy), Lawrene Nixon Anfinson, Thomas Ford, and Hugh Carter. (The descendants of recent Presidents tend to shy from the limelight.) Three nights before the event, only Reagan was unrepresented. His own children either were busy or could not be reached. A telephone call to a historian turned up the telephone number of another historian, who knew of a handful of Reagan cousins in Illinois and Tennessee. After several calls around the country, I reached Karen Dennis, in Baltimore, at midnight. Although she was in the midst of moving houses, she finally agreed to come to New York that weekend, and completed our roster of descendants representing all forty Presidents.

Our descendant coalition was a "great" group: 78 "greats," in fact. Thirteen came from New York, six from Virginia, five from Massachusetts, and the others from as far away as California, Texas, Colorado, Florida, Vermont, and Toronto, Canada—some flew in and out that very day. We had four lawyers, three stockbrokers, three corporation presidents and CEOs, four actors, three teachers, one high-school senior, two museum curators, one ex-destroyer captain, and one rhythm-and-blues musician. Two still live in the homes of their Presidential forebears.

Descendants and Collateral Descendants of the Presidents of the United States

1. George Washington — JOHN AUGUSTINE WASHINGTON, *great great great great great nephew*
   1a. LACEY WASHINGTON, *great great great great great great niece*
   1b. CLEMENT E. CONGER, *descendant of Washington's grandmother*
2. John Adams — CHARLES FRANCIS ADAMS, *great great great grandson*
3. Thomas Jefferson — JOHN WORKS, JR., *great great great great great grandson*
4. James Madison — GRANVILLE GRAY VALENTINE, *great great great nephew*
5. James Monroe — MONROE RANDALL HOES, *great great great grandson*
6. John Quincy Adams — BENJAMIN C. ADAMS, *great great great grandson*
7. Andrew Jackson — ANDREW JACKSON VI, *great great great grandson*
8. Martin Van Buren — HILLES MORRIS TIMPSON, *great great granddaughter*
   8a. T. MICHAEL MARTIN, *great great great great grandson*
9. William H. Harrison — SUSAN HARRISON HENDRYX, *great great great granddaughter*
10. John Tyler — HARRISON RUFFIN TYLER, *grandson*
11. James K. Polk — MILBRY CATHERINE POLK, *great great great great niece*
12. Zachary Taylor — HONORABLE HELEN MARIE TAYLOR, *descendant of Taylor's great great grandfather*
    12a. HOWELL L.T.D. TAYLOR, *Descendant of Taylor's great grandfather*
13. Millard Fillmore — ROBERT FILLMORE NORFLEET III, *great great great nephew*
14. Franklin Pierce — KEN KOOYMAN, *great great great nephew*
15. James Buchanan — JAMES BUCHANAN HENRY IV, *great great great nephew*
16. Abraham Lincoln — CAPTAIN HORATIO A. LINCOLN, USN (Retired), *descendant of Lincoln's uncle*
    16a. ROBERT ADAMS LINCOLN, *descendant of Lincoln's uncle*
17. Andrew Johnson — THOMAS C. COLT, *great great great grandson*
18. Ulysses S. Grant — ULYSSES GRANT DIETZ, *great great grandson*
19. Rutherford B. Hayes — WEBB COOK HAYES III, *great grandson*
20. James A. Garfield — ELIZABETH NEWELL GARFIELD, *great great granddaughter*
21. Chester A. Arthur — JESSIE JACKSON BATCHELLER COGSWELL, *great great niece*
22, 24. Grover Cleveland — GROVER CLEVELAND AMEN, *grandson*
23. Benjamin Harrison — BENJAMIN HARRISON WALKER, *grandson*
25. William McKinley — LYNDA JEANNETTE MCKINLEY MEEK, *great great great niece*
26. Theodore Roosevelt — THEODORE ROOSEVELT IV, *great grandson*
27. William H. Taft — WILLIAM HOWARD TAFT III, *grandson*
    27a. LLOYD BOWERS TAFT, JR., *great grandson*
28. Woodrow Wilson — ELEANOR SAYRE, *granddaughter*
    28a. ELIZABETH SAYRE, *great granddaughter*
29. Warren G. Harding — GEORGE T. HARDING, *great nephew*
    29a. CAROLYN HARDING, *great great niece*
30. Calvin Coolidge — ERMINIE L. POLLARD, *2nd cousin*
    30a. PAMELA SAXTON, *3rd cousin*
31. Herbert C. Hoover — ANDREW HOOVER, *grandson*
32. Franklin D. Roosevelt — DAVID B. ROOSEVELT, *grandson*
    32a. CHANDLER ROOSEVELT, *great granddaughter*
33. Harry S. Truman — MARGARET TRUMAN DANIEL, *daughter*
34. Dwight D. Eisenhower — ANNE EISENHOWER, *granddaughter*
35. John F. Kennedy — ROBIN LAWFORD, *niece*
36. Lyndon B. Johnson — LUCI BAINES JOHNSON, *daughter*
    36a. REBEKAH JOHNSON NUGENT, *granddaughter*
37. Richard M. Nixon — LAWRENE NIXON ANFINSON, *niece*
38. Gerald R. Ford — DR. THOMAS GERALD FORD, JR., *nephew*
39. Jimmy Carter — HUGH CARTER, *1st cousin*
40. Ronald Reagan — KAREN E. DENNIS, *3rd cousin*

GAMMA LIAISON/JOHN CHIASSON

Descendants of all forty-one presidents gathered at Fraunces Tavern on the morning of April 30, 1989.

The President's Ball at the Waldorf-Astoria

More than eight hundred guests attended The President's Ball commemorating the two hundredth anniversary of the inauguration of George Washington, which took place on Sunday evening at the Waldorf-Astoria Hotel in New York City. The ball's honorary chairmen were Mr. and Mrs. Joseph H. Flom and Mr. and Mrs. Milton Petrie. The event's chairmen were Steven J. Ross, the Hon. and Mrs. Herbert Brownell, Mr. and Mrs. Zachary Fisher, and Mr. and Mrs. Ronald Perelman. The event was co-ordinated by George Trescher Associates. Susan Butler of Skadden, Arps, Slate, Meagher & Flom also played a principal role in co-ordinating the event.

After the playing of the National Anthem and a prayer, the program opened with the West Point Glee Club's rendition of the Armed Forces Medley and the "Battle Hymn of the Republic." Mr. Flom then delivered a brief welcoming message, followed by the performance of two musical numbers by a group from the CityKids Foundation. Other speakers included Mayor Koch; "George Washington," who bade farewell to New York City; and Senator Alfonse D'Amato, who proposed a toast to the health of President Bush. The evening's principal entertainment was a performance by Leslie Uggams and Howard McGillin of selections from the Cole Porter musical "Anything Goes." Mr. Flom's closing remarks concluded the formal program.

RONALD L. GLASSMAN

City Commission chairman Joseph H. Flom shares a few words with Mayor Edward I. Koch during the President's Ball at the Waldorf-Astoria. Later, actor William Sommerfield, portraying George Washington, addresses the guests.

PHOTOS: RONALD L. GLASSMAN

Leslie Uggams (right) and Howard McGillan, stars of Cole Porter's "Anything Goes," performed selections from the show.

A lively group of singers from the City Kids Foundation performed at the President's Ball held at the Waldorf-Astoria on Sunday, April 30, 1989.

Federal Hall National Memorial was built as the U.S. Customs House in 1842 on the site of the original Federal Hall which served as the nation's first capitol building from April 1789 to August 1790. At this site Washington was sworn in as President of the United States and Congress proposed the Bill of Rights to the States.

9

The Legacy of the Bicentennial: The Museum of American Constitutional Government

As part of the Commemorative Inaugural Ceremony on April 30, President Bush and the other assembled dignitaries dedicated The Museum of American Constitutional Government at Federal Hall National Memorial. The Museum is a project of the Constitutional Education Foundation, headed by John L. Bryant, Jr., in co-operation with the National Park Service. It is the City Commission's permanent commemoration of the 200th anniversary of George Washington's inauguration, just as the Washington Square Arch was the permanent legacy of the 1889 Centennial celebrations. The City Commission's Legacy Committee, led by Frederick A.O. Schwarz, Jr., and Patrick Mulhearn, was instrumental in establishing the Museum. The design of the exhibits and the educational programs have been developed by American History Workshop, Brooklyn, New York, headed by Dr. Richard Rabinowitz.

The Museum marks a new era in the rich history of this site. The original Federal Hall, which had been built in 1699-1701 as the first City Hall for New York City, was torn down in 1812. The building now known as Federal Hall National Memorial was built by the United States government in 1842. Originally a customs house and then a Sub-Treasury, the building is now a National Memorial maintained by the National Park Service.

The Museum of American Constitutional Government, and its educational arm *The Constitution Works,* combine hands-on and state-of-the-art exhibition techniques to explore the significant historical events that took place at Federal Hall, the process of launching the new government under the Constitution, and the government of New York City. The education program provides junior and senior high school students with a method for understanding the relevance of the Constitution to their own lives. The students use judicial opinions and legislative records, as well as the text of the Constitution, as they play roles in scenarios illustrating the processes of the three branches of government.

The Constitution Works began classes on May 1, with its first curriculum unit —a hypothetical Supreme Court case entitled *Denver Dispatch v. United States.* The curriculum explores whether the First Amendment protects the right of a newspaper to publish sensitive information about national security. During the following six weeks, over 1,000 students from 40 schools throughout New York City came to Federal Hall to play the role of Supreme Court justice or eminent attorney. Since the summer of 1989, *The Constitution Works* has added a second curriculum unit—a hypothetical Senate hearing on a bill called The Excellence and Equal Opportunity Act. This unit offers students the chance to role play a Senate debate on whether gender discrimination in high school athletics violates the equal protection of the laws guaranteed by the Fourteenth Amendment. *The Constitution Works* will soon add a third unit, in which students will learn about the Executive branch.

An essential element of *The Constitution Works* program consists of teacher workshops. Dozens of teachers who want to lead their students through the program can come to Federal Hall to receive special training on the Constitution and on how to lead the role playing exercises. *The Constitu-*

tion Works staff also go out to city high schools to conduct workshops for teachers. After completing the workshop and signing up for the program, teachers receive a full set of classroom materials, including a lesson book for each student and a lesson-by-lesson teacher guide. The printed materials are supplemented by "Constitution Tools"—a short video that dramatizes some of the events used by the students during role-playing.

In addition to the education program, "The Constitution Works" also sponsors other programs at Federal Hall. It produces temporary exhibits on such topics as the government of New York City. The first exhibit, "A New Constitution for New York," dealt with the recently enacted change in New York's City charter. The second exhibit is about the 1990 census—in particular, the difficulties of conducting the census in New York, and its importance to the city. Federal Hall is also the site for special conferences for high school students on Constitutional issues. On September 25, 1989, over 130 New York high school seniors met to commemorate the bicentennial of the passage of the Bill of Rights by the First Congress, meeting at Federal Hall. In April of 1990, *The Constitution Works* will sponsor a conference on the Constitution and the Environment, as part of the celebration of the twentieth anniversary of Earth Day. In addition, *The Constitution Works* is planning a full range of events for the public—from lunchtime lectures to meetings of community groups.

The programs offered by *The Constitution Works* make the Museum of American Constitutional Government unique. Visitors to Federal Hall are participants—in activities that show how our daily lives are shaped by the Constitution.

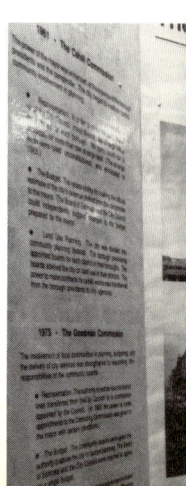

ANNE MAHER

MICHAEL ANTON

MARGARET MAHER

The Museum of American Constitutional Government is the Bicentennial Commission's permanent legacy. Pictured here are the activities of the Museum's educational arm The Constitution Works—which provides junior and senior high school students with a method for understanding the relevance of the Constitution.

10

The Bicentennial: in Perspective*

THE bicentennial of George Washington's inauguration is an appropriate occasion to reflect on the significance of such historical commemorations in the public life of the nation; on the light shed by the bicentennial on our national character, values, and beliefs; and on the lessons that the bicentennial may hold for future generations of Americans. This chapter is a preliminary contribution to that end.

★ ★ ★

THE LARGER CONTEXT

The bicentennial of Washington's inauguration was a stage of the commemoration of the bicentennial of the Constitution. That context gave rise to significant difficulties in planning the celebrations for April 1989.

*This essay by Richard B. Bernstein, the City Commission's historian, represents only his views and not those of the New York City Commission on the Bicentennial of the Constitution. Mr. Bernstein wishes to acknowledge the valuable observations and insights of Joanne B. Freeman, Program Coordinator, Congress Bicentennial Program, Library of Congress.

First, the mere duration of the Bicentennial—in terms of public events, from the fall of 1986 through April 1989—helped to sap the interest of the public and the news media. There are precedents for such "bicentennial exhaustion." For example, as historian Karal Ann Marling has shown in her 1988 study George *Washington Slept Here,* the seven-year binge of patriotic hoopla which Representative Sol Bloom presided over from 1932 to 1939 had results precisely the opposite from the celebrations' intended effect on national pride and morale. Moreover, the commemoration of the bicentennial of the American Revolution in 1974-76 had similar results. It was only natural for most Americans to think that they had been subjected to a continual barrage of bicentennial celebrations for fifteen years.

More than the apparent interminability of the Bicentennial eroded public interest. The most likely cause of "bicentennial exhaustion" was the general incomprehension why there should be so many bicentennials in the first place.

The creation of the American republic does not reduce to one tidy event, easily understood and packaged, photogenic and marketable. The United States and its government were the products of a political process spanning decades and characterized as much by contingency, trial and error, and unforeseen consequences as by political creativity and statesmanship. The scholarly consensus on these points, however, had little in common with the view of the Constitution's origins held by the general public and animating most bicentennial commemorations.

Most bicentennial planners sought to convey the "Miracle at Philadelphia" version of the making of the Constitution—saintly Founding Fathers struggling, in an intellectual and political vacuum, to write a charter of government that at the same time was divinely inspired. This version is misleading, both as constitutional history and as a basis for an intelligent public understanding of the document's origins. Emphasizing the achievement of the Founding Fathers and denigrating their historical context, it lifts constitution-making and nation-building to an Olympian level beyond the capacity of human beings. Just as important, by closing the story of the making of the Constitution with the signing of the document in 1787, this version dismisses the shaping of our constitutional development by individuals and groups who were denied access to the political process in the Founding Period.

Many bicentennial organizers, led by former Chief Justice Burger, described the celebrations as a "history and civics lesson for all of us." This claim makes two assumptions—first, that this "lesson" will spur us to more thoughtful and useful exercise of our political rights and responsibilities; second, that the substance of the "lesson" is properly designed to that end. However, scholars surveying Bicentennial celebrations, public programs, and commemorative publications found little cause for satisfaction.

The national Commission on the Bicentennial was the target of extensive criticism from the scholarly community and the news media. The Commission seemed more interested in staging media events than in educating the public about the history and principles of the Constitution or in drawing on the expertise of historians of the period. As a result, the events planned by the national Commission often flew in the face of prevailing scholarly understandings of the Revolutionary, Confederation, and early national periods, and in the process perpetuated hoary myths and errors of fact. Thus, the work of the national Commission tended to undercut Chief Justice Burger's stated goal of "a history and civics lesson for all of us;" its lesson-plan was deeply flawed.

The bicentennial of the Constitution coincided with another disturbing phenomenon: the American people's growing disenchantment with politics, manifest in declining rates of voter participation at all levels and in dropping levels of confidence in elected officials and the political process. Thus, it was not surprising that the commemoration of some of the central events in our political history evoked little enthusiasm in a populace losing interest in politics. Again, none of this is new. Michael Kammen's 1986 study, *A Machine That Would Go of Itself,* demonstrated that national ignorance or misunderstanding of the Constitution, its history, and its basic principles has been a constant, if previously unrecognized, theme of American history almost since the document's writing and ratification.

In sum therefore, the general problems afflicting the celebration of the Constitution's bicentennial made it more difficult for the planners of the April 1989 celebrations to muster public interest in the anniversary of Washington's inauguration.

Added to these problems was another, more specific obstacle: George Washington is the American historical figure who is least accessible to the American people. This point is a commonplace in Washington scholarship, prompting apologias by virtually every major biographer and historian working on the first President. Marling's *George Washington Slept Here* brought out this difficulty most clearly in her examination of the commemorations in 1932 of the bicentennial of Washington's birth and in 1939 of the sesquicentennial of his inauguration. By that period, she argued, Washington had become so distant and unreal a historical figure, so much the prisoner of the legends accumulating around his life, that he had lost his humanity. The 1987-89 commemorations substantiated Marling's argument. This difficulty made itself felt most dramatically for bicentennial planners at the September 1988 Mount Vernon conference to plan the recreation of Washington's journey in 1789. On that occasion, despite the pleas of the "historiography working group" that the commemoration avoid the overidealizing of George Washington, former Chief Justice Burger declared that he did not see how one could overidealize "this greatest man in our history."

Cross-Purposes: Substance Versus Spectacle

Yet another difficulty faced by the planners of the April 1989 commemoration was the conflict between the desire to present a commemorative program that respected historical accuracy and the need to ensure that the audience for that program—both the public and the news media—would find the events entertaining. Scholars who have taken part in planning commemorations of national anniversaries regularly complain about the sacrifice of substance to spectacle, and have done so at least since the George Washington commemorations of the 1930s. The Civil War Centennial of 1861-1865 and the American Revolution Bicentennial of 1974-1976 illustrate this tendency, as does the recent flurry of television mini-series and docudramas purporting to tell the stories of major historical characters or events.

The City Commission had to face this issue at the beginning of its efforts to plan the April 1989 events. Some Commissioners attacked what they saw as efforts to replace serious discussion of history and modern issues with spectacle. After vigorous discussion of the question, the City Commission concluded that a judicious mixture of substance and spectacle was the only formula with a good chance both to attract the interest of the public and the news media and to communicate some substantive understanding of the events being commemorated.

The City Commission and Radio City Music Hall Productions sought to strike a balance between substance and spectacle. This effort was not uniformly successful. Despite the efforts of the City Commission staff, for example, the script of the Fireworks Spectacular presented the preservation of the Union and the Constitution as the sole achievement of President Abraham Lincoln (an honor which, as many passages in Lincoln's writings indicate, Lincoln never would have claimed for himself). The script also extolled President John F. Kennedy as a principal leader and inspirer of the movement for civil rights, thereby contradicting the arguments both of Kennedy's leading biographers and of the Pulitzer Prize-winning history by Taylor Branch, *Parting the Waters: America in the King Years, 1954-1963*.

The single most difficult case of substance *versus* spectacle was whether or not to re-enact Washington's inauguration. Almost from the day when the national Commission on the Bicentennial took note of the impending anniversary, former Chief Justice Burger endorsed the proposal. The re-enactment of the inauguration loomed over the September 1988 Mount Vernon conference, with the former Chief Justice extolling a full-scale re-enactment as the logical culmination of the re-enactment of Washington's journey from Mount Vernon to New York City. The issue cast a shadow over all subsequent dealings between the national and City Commissions.

Several scholars who were participants at the Mount Vernon conference argued against a re-enactment on the following grounds: *First,* a re-enactment is not history, no matter what claims are made for it and no matter who makes the claims. It can only be a replication of history. *Second,* a re-enactment cannot recreate historical events exactly or, in many cases, even approximately. This is true for many reasons, among them our lack of detailed knowledge about what took place and our need to rely on imperfect, incomplete, and often contradictory accounts of such events. In addition, a faithful re-enactment, approaching as nearly as possible our knowledge of the event as it originally happened, is liable to try the patience and attention of a modern audience. *Third,* because we cannot know exactly what happened, and because modern attention-spans tend to militate against our recreating what we know to have happened, a re-enactment too often becomes a sanitized version of history—history as the re-enactors want it to have happened—at the expense of historical accuracy. Moreover, the message of such a sanitized re-enactment often misses the actual historical significance of the event being re-enacted. *Fourth,* a re-enactment can look ridiculous if accidents mar the scheduled events, or if the planners of the events do not pay sufficient attention to historical detail.

On the evening of April 29, 1989, historian Joanne B. Freeman was present at a cocktail party given by former Attorney General Herbert Brownell (a member of the national and City Commissions on the Bicentennial) in honor of former Chief Justice Burger. What she witnessed on her departure suggests the pitfalls (and pratfalls) on which re-enactments can come to grief:

> I stepped outside the apartment building ...just in time to see George Washington himself step out of a taxicab. He was struggling to look dignified as he tried to realign his ceremonial sword, but he looked so out of place. With a solemn *and somewhat smug acknowledgement of onlookers, GW stepped inside to munch on steak tartare and sip champagne in fluted glasses.... [He] looked somehow simultaneously smug, intimidating, formal, and completely out of place. What in the world was being enacted here? I thought at that moment that I was a witness to the silliest spectacle I had ever seen.*

The City Commission finally agreed to a dramatization of the inauguration, rather than a full-scale re-enactment. This dramatization, limited to ten minutes, was intended to evoke the events of 1789 rather than to recreate them. It was too much to ask of a modern audience to endure a moment-by-moment re-enactment of the actual inaugural ceremony, plagued as it was by delays and miscues, or to sit through the entire text of Washington's inaugural address. In the end, the dramatization took place as described in Chapter VIII. Unfortunately, even this dramatization was marred by avoidable lapses —most notably, the playing of the "March of the British Grenadiers" as the musical accompaniment to "Washington's" arrival. (This lapse was especially regrettable, as the march composed by William Reinagle in 1789 for Washington's arrival in Trenton during his trip to New York City would have been especially appropriate music for the dramatization of the inauguration.) Another mistake was the deletion from the abridged inaugural address of the only substantive recommendation made by Washington—the new President's endorsement of adding a bill of rights to the Constitution.

Nonetheless, and to the surprise of several planners of the commemoration, the dramatization captured the popular imagination and the attention of the news media. Much of the credit belongs to William Sommerfield, whose masterly portrayal of George Washington won over not only the general public and the news media but historians as well. When his carriage arrived at Federal Hall, the audience cheered him as sincerely and enthusiastically as the assembled citizens welcomed the real George Washington two centuries before. Some observers noted that the ticketed audience's decision to rise to their feet as "George Washington" stepped from his carriage was both pragmatic—driven by the desire to see better—and an instinctive echoing of the emotions stirring the original audience of 1789.

Another successful re-enactment was not conceived as a re-enactment: the commemorative service at St. Paul's Chapel (described in Chapter VIII). Again, Joanne B. Freeman:

All the symbolism, staged formality, and awkward groping for proper etiquette was an exact mirror of events of 200 years ago, but an unconscious *one. On April 30, 1789, the new President entered St. Paul's Chapel, accompanied by neck-craning, tense anticipatory excitement, and awkward groping for whether to stand or sit. The service we attended in 1989 was unquestionably contemporary, including references to AIDS and the homeless. But the true emotion of the moment, experienced in the same way that someone might have experienced it 200 years ago, was a reenactment in the finest sense of the word. I truly felt as though somehow I had been touched by some small fragment of the past....*

ADVICE FOR PLANNERS OF FUTURE COMMEMORATIONS AND RE-ENACTMENTS

The commemoration of Washington's inauguration suggests several important features of re-enactments:

First, a re-enactment is of great value to the news media in covering a historical commemoration because it is visually attractive and exciting. It is also useful to the news media because it provides precisely the sort of pageantry that easily communicates the historical nature of the event being commemorated. If well-planned, a re-enactment can be both entertaining and edifying, providing attractive spectacle for the media and the public and bringing alive the essential truth and significance of the historical event being commemorated.

Second, it suggests guidelines for planning a re-enactment as the centerpiece of a historical commemoration. A historical commemoration should give its audience a sense of the history being commemorated and of why that history is worth observing. There will always be grounds for dispute between those who stage such public events and those who, as historians, are enlisted as experts in planning the events, although there is no hard-and-fast rule governing whether and when event-planners or experts should prevail.

Nonetheless, both event-planners and experts should keep certain key points in mind: Historical myths are obstacles to historical understanding, as is sanitizing or distorting the past in order to glorify it and the nation. Make an effort to get the facts as straight as possible, because the history recounted in the re-enactment is likely to be the only historical account of the events being commemorated that the audience will carry away with them.

Nonetheless, the success of the 1989 commemoration of Washington's inauguration indicates that commemorations of historical events, with due regard for the competing claims of historical accuracy and the expectations of the audience and the news media, can make valuable contributions to the American people's understanding of their history. As Joanne B. Freeman concluded after witnessing the 1989 celebration,

Successful public historians can pierce the fog of detail and facts to the core of meaning for the public, and can communicate the 'gut-level' human dimension of the events being commemorated in ways accessible to anyone.

...nstitution

Jack David, Esq.
Chairman, Bar Association Committee on the Bicentennial Association of the Bar of the City of New York

Alfred W. DiTolla
President, International Alliance of Theatrical State Employees and Moving Picture Machine Operators, New York, NY

Olga Diaz
Vice President, Textile Workers Union of America, New York, NY

Howard R. Dressner, Esq.
Shereff, Friedman, Hoffman and Goodman, New York, NY

Zachary Fisher
Fisher Brothers, New York, NY

Anne Sutherland Fuchs
Vice President & Publisher, Women's Day, New York, NY

Eugene A. Gaer, Esq.
Vice President & General Counsel, FOJP Services Corporation, New York, NY

Hon. Norman Goodman
County Clerk, New York County

Jerome L. Green, Esq.
New York, NY

Dr. Vartan Gregorian
President and CEO, The New York Public Library, New York, NY (to February 1989)

James Hoge
President and Publisher, New York Daily News

Dr. Carlos Hortas
Dean of Humanities & Arts, Hunter College, New York, NY

Dr. Czeslaw Karkowski
New York, NY

Diane Kemelman
Administrative Assistant, NYC Corporation Counsel

Arthur Liman, Esq.
Paul, Weiss, Rifkind, Wharton & Garrison, New York, NY

Norman Liss, Esq.
New York, NY

Sister Colette Mahoney
New York, NY

Robert Mahoney
Superintendent of Manhattan Sites, National Park Service

Hon. Barbara Margolis
Commissioner, Mayor's Commission for Protocol

Charles Marshall
Vice Chairman, AT&T, New York, NY

Dr. Marcella Maxwell
Chairperson, NYC Commission on the Status of Women

Dr. Elizabeth P. McCaughey
New York, NY

Harriet Michel
National Minority Supplier Development Council Inc., New York, NY

Michael W. Mitchell, Esq.
Skadden, Arps, Slate, Meagher & Flom, New York, NY

William W. Moore
Director of Municipal Markets, Merrill Lynch Capital Markets, New York, NY

Professor Richard B. Morris
[deceased 1989]
Gouverneur Morris Professor of History, Emeritus, Editor, The Papers of John Jay Columbia University, New York, NY

Thomas Mosser
President, Eastern Division, Burson Marsteller, New York, NY

Hon. Constance Baker Motley
U.S. District Court for the Southern District of New York, New York, NY

Patrick Mulhearn, Esq.
Division Manager — Business Marketing Operations, New York Telephone Company, New York, NY

Carroll (Mrs. Milton) Petrie
New York, NY

Hon. Charles Ramos
Supreme Court — Civil Branch, State of New York, New York, NY

Lewis Rudin
President, Rudin Management Company, New York, NY

Allen G. Schwartz, Esq.
Proskauer, Rose, Goets & Mendelson, New York, NY

Frederick A.O. Schwarz, Jr., Esq.
Cravath, Swaine & Moore, New York, NY

Robert C. Singer
Chairman, George Washington Inaugural Committee, Grand Lodge of Free and Accepted Masons — New York State

Henry Y.S. Tang, Esq.
Brumbaugh, Graves, Donohue and Raymond, New York, NY

John Tobin, Esq.
Dorsey and Whitney, New York, NY

Hon. Peter F. Vallone
Vice Chairman/Majority Leader, Council of City of New York

Ronald Walker
Managing Director, Korn Ferry International, Washington, DC

Hon. Edward Weinfeld
[deceased 1988]
U.S. District Court for the Southern District of New York, New York, NY

...TUTION:

...chwartz
...ffer
...ith

APPENDIX B

Exhibitions and Special Programs

FRAUNCES TAVERN MUSEUM—"The Changing Images of George Washington." February 1—May 28, 1989. This exhibition focused on the way in which American poets, biographers, painters, and printmakers shaped Washington's likeness to reflect the artistic and political eras in which they lived. The exhibition supplemented by a lecture series, and a symposium. A smaller exhibition, "Curiosities," included novel items from the Fraunces Tavern Museum collection related to George Washington. 54 Pearl Street.

MUSEUM OF THE CITY OF NEW YORK—"Celebrating George." February 12—September 10, 1989. This exhibition focused on George Washington, his role in Revolutionary New York, his inauguration, the centennial celebration of his inauguration, and other commemorations; drawing upon the Museum's rich collections of scene paintings and portraits, manuscripts and maps, newspapers, historic prints and photographs, costumes, decorative arts, and toys. Fifth Avenue and 103rd Street.

THE MUSEUM OF BROADCASTING—"The Inaugural Address on Radio and Television." April 14–22, 1989. This screening/listening series included radio and television coverage from the inaugural proceedings of every president since Franklin D. Roosevelt. Each day during the series a different inaugural address was featured. 1 East 53rd Street.

NEW YORK HISTORICAL SOCIETY—"G. Washington in New York." April 27—July 30, 1989. This exhibition drew entirely from the Society's collection of prints, letters, photographs, furniture, and decorative objects documenting Washington's New York years and the city's early celebrations honoring his memory. The Society also sponsored "Government By Choice," a traveling exhibition which visited five sites, one in each borough, from October 1988 through May 1989. 76th St. at Central Park West.

MORRIS-JUMEL MANSION—"Images of George Washington." April 15—July 15, 1989. This exhibition explored Washington's military and political careers, as well as his family life, through 19th and early 20th century prints, personal effects, and memorabilia. The exhibit was designed to give children an in-depth look into the life of George Washington. Morris-Jumel Mansion is Manhattan's oldest remaining residential structure. The house served General Washington as headquarters for the Continental Army in the fall of 1776; he returned to the house in 1790 with members of his presidential cabinet. West 160th Street and Edgecombe Avenue.

GOVERNOR'S ROOM, CITY HALL—A special display of "Washington" artifacts owned by the City of New York was presented by the Art Commission. Paintings, books and Washington's desk from 1789 were all included in this exhibit. Broadway and Murray Street.

TRINITY CHURCH AND ST. PAUL'S CHAPEL—Both sites featured exhibits pertaining to Geroge Washington, his inauguration, and the history of the period. The exhibits were complemented by a lecture and concert series. April 24, 1989-1991.
★St. Paul's Chapel presented "'It Is Done': The Inauguration of George Washington, April 30, 1789." Focusing on the inauguration in 1789 and daily life in the nation's first capital under the Constitution, the exhibition explored the commemoration of the inauguration's centennial in 1889 and its bicentennial in 1989. St. Paul's Chapel, where Washington worshipped after his inauguration in April 1789, is the only structure from that period surviving in lower Manhattan. Broadway and Fulton Street.
★Trinity Church presented: "'An Ocean of Difficulties': The New Nation, 1789-1849," the exhibition presented the first six decades of history and daily life in the new nation. Broadway and Wall St.

UNITED STATES FEDERAL COURTHOUSE—"Birth of a Nation: The First Federal Congress, 1789-1791." This exhibit presented the history of the first Congress to meet under the Constitution. Through reproduced letters, portraits, landscapes, cartoons, and memorabilia, it described key members of that body and chronicled their achievements—including the formation of the executive and judicial branches of the federal government, the proposing of the Bill of Rights, and the formulation of the nation's first economic and fiscal policies. Co-sponsored by the New York State Commission on the Bicentennial of the Constitution and the United States Capitol Historical Society with the assistance of the First Federal Congress Project at The George Washington University and the Second Circuit Committee on the Bicentennial of the U.S. Constitution. Also available was a short history of the First Federal Congress prepared by the First Federal Congress Project with the support of the William Nelson Cromwell Foundation. At Foley Square.

NEW YORK CITY DEPARTMENT OF PARKS AND RECREATION: HISTORIC HOUSES—Sunday, April 16, 1989. The Parks Department sponsored programs at 3 historic houses in northern Manhattan, the Bronx, and Staten Island. These programs included tours, re-enactments, and talks focusing on New York City in the colonial and Revolutionary era.

THE ABIGAIL ADAMS SMITH MUSEUM—Sunday, April 19, 1989. The museum has invited Professor Jacob Judd, Acting Dean of Arts & Humanities at Lehman College, C.U.N.Y., to speak on the topic of "Capital Life: New York City and George Washington's Inauguration." The Abigail Adams Smith Museum is the only historic house in midtown Manhattan. 421 East 61st Street.

NEW JERSEY WATERFRONT MARATHON—Sunday, April 30, 1989. The New Jersey Waterfront Marathon held its annual race on the George Washington Bridge, in celebration of the bicentennial of Washington's inauguration.

WASHINGTON BRIDGE CENTENNIAL—The second oldest working bridge in the City of New York, the Washington Bridge, was opened on April 30, 1989 in commemoration of the Centennial of Washington's inauguration. City officials and community representatives marked the birthday on April 28, 1989 with a special celebration. This impressive steel and iron arch bridge spans the Harlem River, connecting Manhattan at 181st St. with University Avenue in the Bronx.

WASHINGTON INAUGURAL COMMUNITY AWARDS—A program was developed with the New York City Department of Parks and Recreation and the Mayor's Community Assistance Unit to involve neighborhoods throughout the City's five boroughs in the Bicentennial of Washington's Inauguration. Special plantings were dedicated in each of the City's 59 Community Board Districts. The program was kicked off city-wide on Saturday, April 29, "Spring Green-Up Day." Funding for the program was made possible by The Seamen's Bank for Savings.

APPENDIX C

Dais Guests

Hon. Robert Abrams
Attorney General, New York State

Hon. Gary L. Ackerman
Member of Congress

Hon. Donald K. Anderson
Clerk, House of Representatives

Robert Arter
Lieutenant General, U.S. Army (Ret.)

Richard B. Bernstein
Historian, New York City Bicentennial Commission

Hon. Pierre-Louis Blanc
U.N. Ambassador, France

Hon. Lindy Boggs
Member of Congress

Hon. Charles Brieant
Chief Judge, Federal District Court

Rev. Percival Ge. Brown
Trinity Church

Hon. William Holmes Brown
Parliamentarian, U.S. House of Representatives

Hon. Herbert Brownell
Former U.S. Attorney General

Hon. Warren E. Burger
Chairman, U.S. Bicentennial Commission

Hon. George Bush
President of the United States

Barbara Bush
First Lady

Hon. Herbert S. Cables, Jr.
Deputy Director, National Park Service

Rev. Canon Lloyd S. Casson
Vicar, Trinity Church

Hon. Diane M. Coffey
Chief of Staff, Mayor's Office, City of New York

Hon. Philip Crane
Member of Congress

Matthew T. Crosson
Chief Administrator

Hon. Mario Cuomo
Governor, State of New York

Hon. Virenda Dayal
Chief of Cabinet, U.N. Secretary-General

Hon. Miguel I. de Aldasoro
Consul General, Spain

Bob Dornan
Member of Congress

Hon. Becky Norton Dunlop
Assistant Secretary of the Interior

Hon. Benoit d'Aboville
Consul General, France

Hon. Alfonse M. D'Amato
U.S. Senator

Hon. Jan Eliasson
U.N. Ambassador, Sweden

Hon. Wilfred Feinberg
Chief Judge, Federal District Court (Ret.)

Zachary Fisher
Chairman, Intrepid Museum

Joseph H. Flom
Chairman, New York City Bicentennial Commission

Dr. James D. Ford
Chaplain, U.S. House of Representatives

Rabbi Louis C. Gerstein
Temple Shearith Israel

Hon. Harrison J. Goldin
Comptroller, City of New York

Gen. Alfred A. Gray
Commandant, U.S. Marine Corps

Hon. S. William Green
Member of Congress

Helen Hayes

Hon. George J. Hochbrueckner
Member of Congress

Archibishop Iakvos Iakovos
Primate of the Greek Orthodox Church of North and South America

Hon. Adriaan Jacobovits de Szeged
U.N. Ambassador, Netherlands

Hon. Gordon W. Jewkes, CMG
Consul General, Great Britain

Hon. Edward I. Koch
Mayor, City of New York

Hon. Nita M. Lowey
Member of Congress

Hon. Manuel Lujan, Jr.
Secretary of the Interior

Most Rev. Torkom Manoogian
Eastern Diocese, Armenian Church

Hon. John O. Marsh, Jr.
Secretary of the Army

Rev. Dr. Daniel Paul Matthews
Rector, Trinity Church

Rev. William J. McCormak
Auxiliary Bishop, Archdiocese of New York

Hon. Milton Mollen
Presiding Justice, Appelate Division, Second Judicial Department, New York State

Hon. Ames T. Molloy
Doorkeeper, U.S. House of Representatives

Rev. John W. Moody
Trinity Church

Rt. Rev. Paul Moore, Jr.
Bishop, Episcopal Diocese of New York

Hon. Daniel P. Moynihan
U.S. Senator

Father Matthew Mulloy
Church of St. Peter

Hon. Francis T. Murphy
Presiding Justice, Appelate Division

Hon. Manfred Ohrenstein
Minority Leader, NYS Senate

Ronald Perelman
Chairman, Revlon Inc.

John Phelan
President, NY Stock Exchange

Hon. Thomas Pickering
U.S. Representative to the U.N.

Hon. Lawrence W. Pierce
Circuit Judge, Court of Appeals

Hon. Joseph Verner Reed, Jr.
Chief of Protocol, U.S.

Hon. Ned Regan
NY State Comptroller

Hon. James Ridenour
Director, National Park Service

Steven J. Ross
Chairman, Warner Communications

Acknowledgments

We gratefully acknowledge the many people who made valuable contributions to the preparation of WHERE THE EXPERIMENT BEGAN: Joan Stoliar, who designed this book with artistry and industry; Sheri Horn, who helped edit the manuscript with a keen eye for clarity and accuracy; Michael T. Fiur and Peter Nissen, for their valuable special studies included in these pages; Joanne B. Freeman, for her friendly encouragement and for her advice and insight as a historian of the early national period and an observer of the Bicentennial; and William E. Nelson, Professor of Law and History at New York University, who agreed that this project was worth doing.

Without the support of Joseph H. Flom and the generosity of Mr. and Mrs. Milton Petrie and Mr. and Mrs. Zachary Fisher, this book would not exist; we cannot thank them adequately. The same is true of Dr. Stephen L. Schechter, Executive Director of the New York State Commission on the Bicentennial of the United States Constitution, and of his colleague Shirley A. Rice.

We also gratefully acknowledge the assistance of Rett Wallace, Research Assistant, White House Office of Communications; Professor William J. Small and his staff at Fordham University's Graduate School of Business Administration; Michael Fortenbaugh, Manhattan Yacht Club; Terry Dougherty, Fleet Week '89; Zev Trachtenberg and Regan Backer of the Museum of American Constitutional Government at Federal Hall National Memorial; Mary Weir and Linda Reala of Skadden, Arps, Slate, Meagher & Flom; Phyllis Barr of St. Paul's Chapel, Parish of Trinity Church; Shellie Goldberg, The New York Public Library; Carole Slatkin, The New York Historical Society; Patty Smith, New York University; Betty White, Prints and Photographs Division, Library of Congress; Gretchen Diehmann, Museum of the City of New York; and Mina Weiner, guest curator of the exhibition *Celebrating George* at the Museum of the City of New York.

Other friends and colleagues whose aid and counsel made this book possible include Charlene Bickford, Kenneth R. Bowling, and Helen E. Veit of the First Federal Congress Project, George Washington University; Ene Sirvet of *The Papers of John Jay*, Columbia University; Kym S. Rice, historian and curator; John Riley, Archivist/Curator, Mount Vernon Ladies' Association; Roni Schwartz and Rachel Conescu, architects of the "Preambles" program; Jerome Agel; Marvin Kitman, *New York Newsday;* D. Graham Combs, Harper & Row; Phillip Haultcoeur, Bantam Doubleday Dell; Marjorie Mortensen of the Mayor's Office of Special Projects and Events; Marsha Shapiro, for alerting us to Clarence Bowen's 1892 *Centennial History;* and Allan Appel.

Stephanie Adler, Associate Director of the City Commission, and Betty Farrell, the City Commission's office manager, deserve special recognition for their unswerving commitment to the work of the City Commission and the preparation of this history.

P.S.K. AND R.B.B.

*The City Commission on
the Bicentennial sought
not only to commemorate the history
of the 1780s, but to remind us all
that we have a living Constitution.
The making of the Constitution
is a political and legal process
which continues to this day—
a process in which all of us,
not just lawyers and judges
and scholars, play a vital part.*

Joseph H. Flom
*Chairman, New York City Commission
on the Bicentennial of the Constitution*

This book was set in 10 point Bembo
with Caslon Oldstyle #2 display
by Maxwell Typographers, New York City.
It was printed on 70# Mountie Matte
by Hoffman Printing, Buffalo, N.Y.